KEFIR
Rediscovered!

to Frantziska
for better health
with the
champagne
of milks

Canada Place
1 Oct. 2000
Klaus K.

alive books

KEFIR
Rediscovered!
The Nutritional Benefits of an Ancient Healing Food

Klaus Kaufmann
Foreword by Zoltan Rona MD, MSc

alive
books

Published by
Alive Books
PO Box 80055
Burnaby BC Canada V5H 3X1

Designer: Kerstin Barth
Cover Photo: David Jennings
Back Cover Photo: Ron Long

Printing, first edition: April 1997

Canadian Cataloguing in Publication Data

Kaufmann, Klaus, 1942-
Kefir rediscovered!

Includes bibliographical references and index.
ISBN 0-920470-65-3

1. Kefir. 2. Kefir--Therapeutic use. I. Title
RM257.K4K38 1997   641.3'7146   C97-910106-9

Printed and bound in Canada

To my great-grandfather
Johannes Heinrich Bing (modo Kaufmann).
In 1864 he added a stable for keeping goats for fresh milk and cheese
to our house in Bad Neukirchen, Germany,
a 17th century heritage home still in the family

And *thou shalt have* goats' milk enough for thy food,
for the food of thy household,
and *for* the maintenance for thy maidens

HOLY BIBLE
KING JAMES VERSION, PROVERBS 27:27

Contents

Part IV - A Whirl of Recipes

Acknowledgments

No man is an island. My heartfelt thanks to every-one drinking or eating kefir. You made this book pos-sible! To my kefir gurus *Siegfried and Christel Gursche* and *John Donovan*, who are the true novo-creators of kefir, many thanks. Thanks also to my edi-tors *Marion MacLean* and *Kathy Zia*, who made the text worthy of kefir's white resplendence. Any remain-ing errors are mine. My lovely wife of twenty years, *Gabryelle*, diligently lent her even more lovely ears to be my sounding board! And, curled at my feet, our beautiful-of-nature Labrador-Newfoundland *Bing*, better known as "Big Red," rejuvenated me with cool doggie thoughts, while I cooled myself during the hot July and August days of this manuscript's awakening with draught after draught after draught of delicious kefir. Even so, I was late.

Foreword

It's a very good thing we are blessed with the writing and teaching talents of Klaus Kaufmann. His latest book on the wonders of kefir could not have come at a better time. Thanks to the public's overconsumpton of antibiotics, steroid hormones and refined foods, North Americans suffer from an unprecedented epidemic of immune system disorders. We need not look too far to see what the combined efforts of the medical profession, the pharmaceutcal industry, the mercury dental fillng pushers and the agribusiness polluters have done to destroy the health of millions. Thanks to these antagonists (or should I say antaGOONists) of natural healing, we are seeing skyrocketting incidences of Chronic Fatigue Syndrome, asthma, middle ear infections, attention deficit disorder, the candida/yeast syndrome, 20th Century Disease, autoimmune diseases like lupus, rheumatoid arthritis and thyroiditis, AIDS and cancer. Other common disease consequences are chronic bowel disorders like colitis, Crohn's disease and irritable bowel syndrome (IBS), the latter of which is the number one reason why general practitioners refer patients to gastroenterologists (gut specialists).

Antibiotics and steroids are seemingly everywhere. Not only do we get them as prescriptions from well intentioned medical doctors for various infections and inflammations, but we also find them in our commercial dairy products, beef, pork and poultry. Despite the large amounts of antibiotics and hormones pumped into cows, pigs, fish and chickens, studies continue to show that the foods derived from these animals are contaminated with parasites as well as pathogenic bacteria and fungi. Conservative estimates indicate that as many as 80 percent of all North Americans (and this includes government bureaucrats and medical doctors) are contaminated with parasites.

Prescription antibiotics kill off the good, immune enhancing bacteria normally present in our gastrointestinal tracts. Yeast and fungi thrive when friendly bacteria that normally keep them in check in the bowel are wiped out by antibiotics. Our host defences are compromised and the next thing we know, we come down with an infection of some kind. This, of course, for the majority of people, means getting yet another antibiotic prescription from their doctor which leads to further immune suppression secondary to the resulting yeast or fungal infection. Fungi like candida can secrete mycotoxins which further weaken immunity and stimulate cancer and heart disease development. The good news, however, as you are about to read, is that there is something you can do to fight back against all this.

As I write this I am sitting in an airplane on my way to Vancouver to speak at a public forum on freedom of choice in health care issues. In its not so infinite wisdom, the HPB (Health Protection Branch), the Canadian version of the American FDA (Food and Drug Administration), has come down hard on over 60 different herbs and homeopathic remedies, reclassifying them as drugs and making them, for the most part, inaccessible to the public as of Jan. 1, 1997. A great deal of evidence now exists that this is the latest move by the international pharmaceutical-medical complex lead by the Codex Commision (made up mostly by drug company representatives) of the World Health Organization (WHO) to wipe out their perceived competition.

While it may be a noble effort to fight against this sort of government sponsored terrorism, we sometimes forget that, even if we do not have access to bottled vitamins, minerals, melatonin, DHEA and other cure-all supplements, we can still do a great deal to boost our immunity and prevent disease by knowing what to eat. For pennies a day we can prevent and even reverse cancer and other diseases of altered immune function by consuming whole foods like kefir, sauerkraut, flaxseed, kombucha, shiitake, maitake and reishi mushrooms, seaweeds, aloe vera, asparagus, garlic, cruciferous vegetables like broccoli, cauliflower and brussel sprouts and soy products like tempeh, miso and tofu. No doubt, Klaus will rediscover some of these special foods for us in future *Rediscovered Series* books.

Kefir should be especially appealing in these times. Besides its low cost and powerful immune system healing effects, kefir is an excellent source of essential amino acids, enzymes, vitamins, minerals and other "nutraceuticals" currently being scrutinized by government bureaucrats. What's more, you can make kefir in the privacy of your home legally without the intrusion of the HPB (although this remains to be seen in the years to come). Enjoy the many interesting kefir recipes in the last chapter and Klaus' inimitable sense of humor throughout this eye-opening new book.

Here's wishing you rediscover optimal health starting with this book.

—**Zoltan P. Rona MD, MSc**
Author, *Return to the Joy of Health* and
Childhood Illness and the Allergy Connection

The highest, most illustrious, whatever mind unfurled,

Is always plagued by strange and stranger matter;

When finally we achieve the good of this world,

Then fallacy and fad are called the better.[1]

GOETHE

Introduction

There I was in Nashville, Tennessee, the world's haven for country music, to sign copies of my latest book, *Kombucha Rediscovered!*, at the National Nutritional Food Association's annual natural foods show and convention. I felt honored: a long queue had formed, waiting to secure an autographed copy of my latest work—even before my arrival. The trade show crowd was buzzing with healthy enthusiasm. Later, my wrist sore from signing, I joined the throngs of people walking the floors in search of healing foods, foods they and I had not yet discovered—or rediscovered.

I follow Dr. Max Gerson's prescription that *"nutritional therapy be the foundation of all efforts to maintain health and to heal."* Gerson demands that a physician's first act must be to modify the eating patterns of the sick. Food intake and the metabolism must be changed to trigger nature-given healing mechanisms in the diseased. Only then can the doctor create a foundation for successful therapy. The old dictum "Let your foods be your medicine and your medicines be your food," is also kept foremost in my mind. Ever since a wrong medical diagnosis in childhood, I have been a firm believer in looking after my health by way of the foods I eat and nutrients I take in.

But, as was in evidence at the NNFA convention, there seems to be a new paradigm emerging in the health food industry—a return to the "fix me quick doctor!" mentality. It struck me how easily we are led astray. For there amid the great natural food products and the vitamin and mineral supplements, were newly fashioned, newly fabricated, newly synthesized products. These newfangled products are quickly gaining fame under the heading of *nutraceuticals*.

"When is a drug not a drug?" When it's a *nutraceuticals*—a hybrid word describing therapeutics that are made from foods. Are nutraceuticals healing foods? Or are they a new wave of *"ceuticals"* about to replace the pharmaceuticals the health food industry has been up against for decades? Though nutraceuticals are made from foods, they are "refined" and "isolated" much like their pharmaceutical cousins. All is not well in the state of Denmark, especially considering that more and more nutraceuticals with worrisome side effects (like the synthetic hormones melatonin and DHEA) are already being taken by health-seeking consumers.

So, in this context the word "rediscovered" took on new dimensions. For in writing a book about kefir—a traditional food with a long and venerable history—I rediscovered a natural, health-enhancing and delicious product. And I am now convinced that there are many other foods whose remarkable properties are waiting to be viewed in a new light. We have not exhausted nature's bounty, and until we do, nutraceuticals are not really necessary.

Soon her eye fell on a little glass box
that was lying under the table:
she opened it, and found in it a very small cake,
on which the words 'EAT ME' were beautifully marked.

ALICE'S ADVENTURES IN WONDERLAND
LEWIS CARROLL

Part I

QUAFFING KEFIR

Chapter 1

Following the Milky Way

Immortal Cultured Milk

My Goodlife Kefir Maker is working double time. With increasing fascination I watch the milk in the jar atop the refrigerator come alive. Before my eyes a treelike structure is slowly taking shape. I am in the South China Sea, diving into the corals. Then it occurs to me that this awesome coral structure could just as easily be a vegetable structure, a cauliflower floret, for instance. What is blossoming before my eyes is, of course, none of that. The foamy white sculpture is a growing mountain of kefir grains.

Traditional kefir making consists of mixing milk preheated to 80°F (28°C) with kefir grains. The kefir grains start the fermentation process. These grains are convoluted gelatinous particles obtained from fermented milk. They are white to yellow in color and look a little like cauliflower florets or segments of coral. The grains vary from almost not visible to the human eye to hazelnut size. Kefir grains are insoluble in water and common solvents.

This makes kefir grains unique. Because only when added to milk does their size expand and take on moisture. The color of the grains changes

3

into white. Kefir grains then turn ordinary milk into a delicious drink. The grains are generally recoverable and can be repeatedly used. This is a prime advantage of kefir, which, as we will find out by way of a short story, has been perfected and standardized. This makes kefir making simple and easy, much easier than making yogurt.

As can be seen, kefir is a grain with distinction. Actually, it is not a grain at all, but it does have much culture. In fact, kefir (pronounced *key-fur*) is a *cultured milk*, much like buttermilk, no... like quark, no... like yogurt, only much better. Kefir is better in many ways, and we will explore them one by one. I promise you, it'll be fascinating. But up front, I will reveal that the very best reasons for drinking and eating kefir is that it will contribute to your good health and help keep you rejuvenated.

Coming of Age

I know. I am guilty of it myself! We are all forever looking for the remedy, drink or food that will grant us a long and healthy life—let us live forever maybe? No wonder our literature is full of the promise of eternal youth. Dorian Grays, whether through magic paintings, youth elixirs, resurrections, or in a more ghoulish form of the vampire, are ever intriguing. Eternal life, not eternity, is prized and promised. Is it truly attainable for this, our physical body and mind? I think not. No-thing lasts forever, Dr. Deepak Chopra's new age teachings notwithstanding. It is my belief that our souls are truly eternal. But our bodies need not deteriorate until we are ready to leave them for a better world.

My forefathers built our family home several centuries ago. With tender loving care, restoration, and repairs, the Kaufmann house is still standing. Our personal house—our body—can be equally well kept, provided we recognize that it too requires tender loving care, restoration, and repair. Eating and drinking wholesome kefir offers just such care to our physical selves. Kefir can help restore our body to full function and well-being. Kefir, with continued use, will repair many of our ills. While it won't keep us alive forever, it will, in conjunction with other nutritious foods, proper lifestyle and exercise, aid us in our quest for optimal health.

True Health

Ironclad scientific studies (controlled *in vitro* and *in vivo* studies) confirming that kefir is healthy and will keep you youthful well into old age unfortunately do not exist and are not likely to ever exist. Only multi-national pharmaceutical companies can afford to conduct costly double and double-blind studies—and there is nothing for them to gain by proving the effectiveness of kefir. There are, however, a number of scientific studies made that indicate that kefir has many health-enhancing qualities. So, do not despair. The pursuit of true health is, after all, not in need of such modern ways of convincing us that something works. With insight (the study of studying) and common sense (the study of logic) and historical data (the best because it is long term time-exposure study) true ways to health can be found.

The Champagne of Milk

An article in *Dairyfoods Newsletter* by Dairyland, Vancouver, BC, in 1994 called kefir the twenty-first century yogurt. Kefir has a far more interesting taste than yogurt, and different milks will create a variety of mouth watering kefir flavors. Kefir also contains a small amount of alcohol, about one-fifth to one half of one percent (0.2 to 0.5 percent)—a negligible amount that does not preclude its use by children. Yet, like beer and sparkling wines, kefir creates carbon dioxide (CO_2), an effervescent, during fermentation. This does not make kefir foam and fizz, but turns it into a very interesting drink. So, one could say that yogurt is to milk what wine is to grapes, but kefir is to milk what champagne is to grapes, which is why kefir, and not yogurt, is the champagne of milk.

You are no doubt familiar with yogurt. Yet it was not so long ago that the majority of people did not know what yogurt was or looked at it askance. Today, however, yogurt is ubiquitous. It comes in all sorts of colorful flavors and various consistencies. Yet despite the enormous increase in yogurt consumption, few people make yogurt at home. Why? One reason is that yogurt cultures very quickly lose their potency and must be bought repeatedly.

The reverse is true of kefir! The kefir culture is hardier, more potent and can self-generate more easily than a yogurt culture. Kefir regenerates itself constantly. This makes kefir an ideal home brew. Kefir has the additional unique quality of being very tolerant to differing conditions, allowing for its use under a wide range of temperatures, climates and growth mediums.

Here are some other qualities that give kefir an advantage over yogurt:

• Milk used for making kefir does not have to be preheated like milk for making yogurt. This makes it ideal for use with "certified raw milk."

• More on certified raw milk later. For a full explanation of the various types of milks, i.e., standard, raw, homogenized, skim, etc., see page 12.

• Smaller curds make kefir far more digestible than yogurt because enzymes in the digestive tract cling better and more easily to the much larger surface area thus offered, the net result of smaller curds. We'll investigate that more closely, too, but, for instance, in my book *Silica— The Amazing Gel*, I pointed to the similar larger total surface area for enzymatic action offered by smaller particles.

• Kefir is the only fermented milk starter culture that takes the form of ready-for-action grains. These grains grow naturally from lactic acid bacteria, yeasts, casein and a fibrous carbohydrate gum called kefiran. This gum "glues" the resident microflora together into a natural but temporarily immobilized cell system. All it needs to "explode" into life is a drop of milk!

• Kefir contains "right-turning" lactic acid, usually called L+ lactic acid. How turning left vs. turning right makes a huge difference not only on the highways, but in your very own bodily pathways, we will soon know in some detail.

• Perhaps best of all, the cost of making kefir is far below the cost of making yogurt. The kefir culture (unlike any yogurt culture) never dies. Thus, kefir cultures do not have to be bought time and again. Kefir grains are "immortal." Yogurt cultures are merely like "humans," they have a birth, a childhood and youth stage, an adult stage, and sinking-towards-death stage.

And these are just some of the reasons why kefir is unique among soured milks. Besides creating internal harmony and preventing illnesses of the digestive tract, kefir has valuable external applications as well. Why, you can even bathe in it! Kefir cleanses and reconstitutes skin all in one application. And its great effectiveness can be had for next to nothing as you can make your own fantastic soaps and creams at home for mere pennies.

So, you can see that kefir is more than just a healthful drink. Once you make it part of your regular diet, you will know why throughout the centuries kefir has been revered as a refreshing drink, a delicious and healthy food and a restorative with inner and outer applications.

Soured Secrets and the Golden Horde

In the summer, my mother made soured milk for us kids. She would use the very freshest raw milk, which I fetched in a milk can from the milk grocer. Mom poured this foamy milk into glazed ceramic containers or glass bowls. Then she sealed them with kitchen towels and elastics to keep out the bugs. She placed the bowls on the window sill, putting them out of harms way (The harm was boys—I have three brothers.) and added a short prayer of good thoughts. We kids added the good vibrations by making a hullabaloo! Twenty-four hours later we had soured milk for lunch. A drink had become a food. It continued to be what I considered the most delicious way of "eating"milk until I discovered kefir.

The ancient Greeks considered milk and soured milk products a perfect and superior food. And while Napoleon's army was wiped out by the Russian winter, the Golden Horde of Genghis Khan almost conquered all of Europe centuries earlier because their food supply was assured even in the coldest winters of the Russias. The Mongols' rations, you see, included a fermented milk that was in continuous production in leather sacks strapped to their horses.

Fermented food products were most likely discovered by chance. Legend has it that cheese-making was so discovered: A rider on horseback takes along milk for sustenance on route. The milk is stored in a leather pouch attached to the saddle bag. The leather pouch is made from a calf's stomach lining. Calves' stomachs, as you may know, contain a wondrous ferment that makes things curdle. It's called rennet, which in Old English means "run together." The traces of rennet separated the milk solids from the whey, and now the rider found a curd. The curd he unwittingly created is very similar to today's buttermilk or quark.

Kefir Capers from Days of Yore

The presence of fermented dairy products dates back to the earliest civilizations. The Veda, the ancient Sanskrit scriptures of India, makes mention of a fermented milk product called dadhi. Clay tablets from Sumer, our most ancient civilization, record the making of fermented milk. The Bible mentions soured milk.

No one really knows where kefir came from. Some authorities believe kefir originated in Turkey, others think it came from Russia. It doesn't really matter because kefir truly is a Turkish delight and a Russian rapture. Suffice it to say that kefir originated in the northern Caucasus Mountains, where legend has it that kefir grains were given to the orthodox by the prophet Mohammed.

As it was believed that kefir would lose its strength if used by infidels, kefir making was a strictly kept secret. Considered part of the wealth of the family and tribe, kefir grains were passed on through the generations. So it was that the "Grains of the Prophet" were kept secret and away from the rest of the world.

Occasionally, strange tales were heard of an unusual beverage with "magical" properties. And Marco Polo, the famed Venetian world traveler, mentioned kefir in the chronicles of his travels in the East. But kefir continued to be an unknown entity outside the Caucasus for centuries, until news spread of its use in the treatment of tuberculosis and stomach diseases. And while the first scientific studies on kefir were published in Russia at the end of the nineteenth century, there was still no easy or reliable source of kefir grains.

Russian Rapture

The story of how kefir came to Russia is one of intrigue and romance: Having heard of kefir's amazing healing properties, the Russian Physician's Society, at the turn of this century, resolved to obtain kefir and make it available to their patients.

Thus, in the early 1890s[2], the society approached the brothers Blandov[3], who ran a dairy in Moscow and also had a cheese factory in the Caucasus. The plan was to obtain kefir grains and mass-produce kefir in Moscow. To this end, Nikolai Blandov sent a beautiful young employee, Irina Sakharova, to the court of Bek-Mirza Barchorova, a local prince. She was to charm the prince and persuade him to give her some kefir grains. He refused out of respect for religious law that forbade the passing on of kefir grains. Dispirited, Irina and her party left for Moscow.

In the mountains they were suddenly assaulted by tribesmen who kidnapped Irina and returned her to the prince. As it was a local custom to "steal" brides, Irina was told that she was to marry the smitten prince. Only a daring rescue mission staged by her employers saved Irina from that forced marriage. The unlucky prince was summoned to the czar, who ruled that in retribution the prince was to give Irina ten pounds of kefir grains for the insult she suffered at his hand.

These grains made their way to the Moscow Dairy and in September of 1908, the first bottled kefir drink was offered for sale in Moscow. The kefir habit spread quickly, encouraged perhaps by the story of its origin. Finally, in 1973 the Minister of the Food Industry of the then-Soviet Union sent a letter to Irina Sakharova, thanking her for her important role in bringing kefir to the Russian people.

Spice of All the Russias

Today all the regions that comprise the former USSR are makers and con-sumers of kefir. The Russians go all out. Annual per capita consumption in 1977 was 4.5 kg or 10 lb. of kefir per person.[4] Put differently, it accounts for 65 to 80 percent of total fermented milk sales in Russia, which leads the world in kefir technology and is the largest commercial producer.[5]

Russians use milk from all types of farm animals, including cows, sheep and goats, in their advanced kefir formulas. There are other regions in the world, the Far East and Africa mainly, where milk from sheep, water buffaloes, mares and sows is used as well. These milks vary in their makeup of fat, casein, whey protein, lactose and other ingredients.

Nevertheless, any animal milk can be the base for kefir, using the same lac-tic acid fermentation process. Soymilk and most other so-called "milks" can also be soured into kefir products. However, this is not true of rice milk, most likely because it lacks sufficient fat content. But no matter which milk you use, if it has been treated with Ultra Heat, so-called UHT-milk, it will not work. Goes to show you that kefir needs live food to work with.

What's in a Name?

Often enough the most intimate secret of a food is hidden in its very name. Such is the case with kefir—the fundamental nature of which is revealed in its etymology.

The word kefir, sometimes also spelled kefyr, apparently comes from the Turkish word keif, which means "good feeling" or "pleasure." And really, what more could we ask of a drink and food than that it should give us a feeling of well-being after ingesting it?

It has also been suggested that the word kefir is related to the word "kiaf" for "foam" or the Turkish word "kef" for "intoxicating," which is going a bit too far, seeing as how kefir, with so little alcohol, is not. A word common in the Caucasus region is "kefy," and at least one Russian researcher is suggest-ing that it stands for kefir and means "best quality." Well, why not?

Cultured Soymilk:
Not the Twenty-first Century Beverage!

A 1997 report on milk consumption published by the prestigious British Journal of Cancer concludes there is "an overwhelming association between high consumption of milk and prevention of breast cancer." "So,"

I hear some of you say, "that's all fine and dandy, but I cannot digest milk!" And then, with emphasis, "I am lactose intolerant!" You are not alone. Many individuals have trouble digesting lactose or milk sugar. The key to lactose digestion is yet another ferment, mmhhh . . . an enzyme I should say.

Much is made of enzymes. What are they? They used to be called ferments. Indeed, they are ferments still as they bring about fermentation. The words 'ferment' and 'enzyme' are interchangeable. Typically though a ferment is an 'enzyme' (from Greek for leavening!) when it is an organic and action-specific catalyst that is produced by a living cell and speeds up specific chemical reactions. The older traditional ferments are the bacteria, molds and yeasts. Yet, as we now know, they also create enzymes to bring about fermentation outside the body.

To digest lactose, the human digestive system must convert, e.g., ferment lactose into something else. A body enzyme called lactase enables this process by making haste. This lactose-fermenting enzyme allows the digestive tract to split lactose into smaller constituents and easily absorb it. People whose metabolism cannot synthesize the lactase enzyme lose out on much of milk's carbohydrate energy. Worse, the lactose they consume in milk can stay undigested and unabsorbed in their digestive tract and there accumulate to problematic levels. In really sensitive individuals this causes diarrhea, abdominal pains and cramps. Undigested lactose also tends to interfere with the friendly intestinal bacteria. It's worth noting then, that kefir fermentation converts most of the lactose in ordinary milk into far more easily digested components, and of course alcohol. The remaining lactose content is so low that most otherwise lactose-intolerant people find that, through kefir, they can enjoy milk again.

Even staunch vegans can enjoy the benefits of kefir. You see, kefir grains work very nicely with soymilk—*unudder* milk. This milk substitute from soybeans contains no lactose. But the real trouble is that cultured or fermented soymilk tastes bad! Yet vegans, who love soymilk, can enjoy the benefit of lactic acid from soymilk even though it tastes quite bland. Still, soymilk provides enhancement of intestinal microflora in ways quite similar to cow's or other animal's milk. Long term, if humans continue to populate the planet at the current rate of reproduction, soymilk may well be the only milk available or affordable even though it is not really the milk of choice. Kefir would then be the only milk fermentation formula of the soy future, leaving yogurt out in the cold.

The Most Sensitive Food

I had always wondered how my mother managed to obtain lactic acid fermentation cultures for her soured milk right after the war—that is until I found out that cow's milk naturally contains lactic acid bacteria. This bacteria, under the right conditions, will cause a spontaneous souring in untreated cow's milk. Mind you, my mother used 'certified raw' or 'standard' milk that was made safe just by cooling it, and thus was not 'killed' in the process.

Milk is one of the most satisfying food substances in the world—every infant of every mammal instinctively knows this. Milk, like no other natural food, contains an ideal blend of all the essential minerals, trace elements, vitamins and growth factors we humans need. It's true! So no wonder milk easily spoils or is easily contaminated.

Its high reactivity to its environment is both a boon and a bane. A major change in weather can quicken the spoilage of milk, even in the seeming safety of the refrigerator. But that very reactivity also leads to an endless variety of delicious-tasting foods that can be made with milk. Just think of the endless variety of cheeses.

Cow's milk consists of 85 to 88 percent water and 3.3 percent proteins. The remaining constituents are organic substances and minerals. There are also small quantities of lactates and citrates and traces of iron and magnesium. The carbohydrates present in milk constitute about 4.8 percent and consist of lactose (milk sugar) and small quantities of other sugars. The amount of fat varies, of course, with the type of milk you are using. Raw milk usually contains up to 3.7 percent of fat. Fat content (or its absence) is always given for the dairy product.

There are also small quantities of stearic acid and short-chain fatty acids. Sterols and phosphatides are also present. The act of churning the milk causes the fat to unite into a solid mass and separates the whey. This action results in butter and buttermilk. While vitamin A and the B-complex are naturally present in adequate quantities for your or your child's needs, milk is naturally low in vitamins C and D. These vitamins are often added for this reason.

Natural souring of milk occurs if left standing at room temperature because of the natural presence of lactic acid bacilli converting lactose to lactic acid. When the milk's pH reaches 5.34, coagulation occurs and with it the production of curd. Milk also contains natural antibodies and a number of enzymes.

Reanimating Exanimate Milk

Because of its environmental sensitivity, and to preclude the sale of milk from unhealthy animals, the government long ago assumed control over how we receive our milk. Under governmental supervision, milk intended for distribution is cleansed and pasteurized. In some countries and regions milk is also irradiated to kill off microbes such as tuberculosis, coli, paratyphus or streptococci. There is also specially treated milk that is quickly heated to 300°F (150°C) and then super-quickly cooled. Such milk can be stored at room temperature for at least six weeks without spoiling.

In pasteurization, milk is gently heated to 144°F (62°C) for 30 minutes. Alternatively, it may be "flash" heated to a higher temperature for less than one minute. Both processes are equally effective for removing unwanted bacteria without changing the chemical composition. Just how effective? Pasteurization removes unwanted bacteria by 97 to 99 percent. Pasteurization is so efficient because the common milk-borne pathogens do not form spores and are quite sensitive to heat. Before pasteurization, contaminated milk often caused serious disease. However, pasteurization also changes milk. No more live lactic acid bacteria can be found, which is why such milk cannot be soured the way my mother soured milk for us kids.

Then there is homogenization. This process emulsifies the milk by subjecting it to heat under pressure. It results in a semi-permanent mixing of fat globules and casein particles and renders milk uniform. Especially lately, the value of homogenization has been greatly questioned by scientific, nutritional and medical experts. The milk available in stores is also classified according to fat content. Thus one will find whole or homogenized (no fat removed), two percent (some of fat removed) and skim (virtually fat-free). These milks all have a limited shelf life even under refrigeration and will spoil very quickly under ordinary room temperature.

Lactic acid-ferments contain antibacterial properties that control the attack of pathogens on the milk, thereby increasing shelf life a little. Yet one of the greatest boons that kefir bestows on ordinary milk is that its lactic acid bacteria reanimate the milk and put the life back into treated and therefore deadened milk. But, can we perhaps obtain raw certified milk that is left untreated for our kefir? Let's see.

In Search of Raw Certified Milk

When making kefir, the freshness and quality of the milk you use is vital. If you live in the Provinces of British Columbia or Alberta in Canada, a good way to ensure this is to buy milk in glass bottles. Avalon Dairy Ltd. of

Vancouver is one dairy that uses glass bottles; Royal Oak Dairy on Vancouver Island is another. I have heard also of such a dairy in Quebec, and am quite sure that milk in glass bottles is available in most provinces as well as in the United States.

Avalon Dairy assures me that not only does their milk taste better because of being in glass bottles, it also keeps better and stays fresher longer. Avalon sells all kinds of milks in glass bottles, i.e., standard, homo, 2%, etc. In addition, Avalon regularly tests all of their milk for antibiotics. By law, in British Columbia, dairy farmers may not administer hormones to dairy cows. Best of all, Avalon carries a type of "certified raw milk" called standard milk, which contains 3.25 percent butterfat.

This fat usually floats on top of the milk; a sign that the milk is not homogenized. Avalon's standard milk is the closest thing to milk as the cow produced it, with nothing added and nothing skimmed off. Such milk is the most excellent for making kefir, except, of course, for certified raw milk.

In a work I will call in translation "The Botched-Up Job with the Milk 6," well-known German authors Dr. med. M. O. Bruker and Dr. phil. Mathias Jung cite many great reasons for returning to the days of raw milk, such as the fact that bacteria present in raw milk are both harmful and beneficial and how the beneficial get killed with the harmful in modern milk processing. Yet certified raw milk is—to the best of my knowledge, and please let me know of other sources!—only available in the USA State of California, being sold by Alta Dena Dairies, who reside in the City of Industry. Of course, even certified raw milk will have been pasteurized, as this is required by law. All other milks, including other Avalon milks, are also homogenized.

In view of antibiotic pasteurization, there is evidence that antibiotic properties are produced in milk during kefir fermentation. Of course, the lactic acid, acetic acid and hydrogen peroxide in the fermented milk already tend to inhibit organisms that induce spoilage. Other antimicrobial components produced by lactic acid bacteria are called bacteriocins. These are extracellular protein peptides that cannot be artificially made. They are "bactericidal" to a wide range of pathogens. They are more potent than antibiotics with a narrower, more focused, range. According to E. Schneider, MD, soured milk like kefir, containing bacteriocins, is prescribed by doctors in Germany for patients suffering from obesity, chronic constipation, skin problems, stomach disorders and intestinal diseases. It so happens that the friendly bacteria in kefir, once resident in the intestines, act as watchdogs by keeping an eye on, and effectively controlling, the spread of undesirable microorganisms. The kefir bacteria achieve this by altering the acidity of the region they inhabit. They also control rival "unfriendly" bacteria by depriving them of sustenance.

Dr. Schneider ascribes the healing action of kefir to the ingredients of lactic acid and the living lactic bacteria. Lactic acid performs digestive tasks similar to those of hydrochloric acid or other bodily digestive juices, thereby easing the digestive burden. Schneider also points to soured milk as a great tonic for people suffering from weak nerves because of the great amount of lecithin in soured milk.* In holistic medicine, milk therapy plays a major role in the treatment of liver ailments, particularly of jaundice. Milk therapy is also useful in diets designed for overcoming stomach and duodenal ulcers. As well, heart patients suffering from the additional burden of water accumulation in the tissues (edema) can obtain quick relief from a highly specialized milk. Known as Karell Therapy in Germany, the patient's only permitted food intake is one liter of milk per day. So, as you can see, milk, particularly in the form of kefir, is a wide-ranging healing agent.

The Trouble with Cultured Milks on Store Shelves

Many of the cultured milks on supermarket shelves are devoid of natural cultures and are therefore devoid of the beneficial properties that natural fermentation bestows.

Such products are made by a process that uses direct acidification instead of lactic cultures. While this achieves easier processing and allows for a consistent product and increased product longevity, it is at the expense of nutrient value. Consequently, we must be wary of commercial cultured milks that contain many mixed organisms. Some yogurts do not even mention what is in them, finding it sufficient to print "contains live cultures." Yeah? Which ones? But there is one way of making sure that you receive the many benefits of cultured milk products: make your own kefir. It is a very simple process, as you will see. But first we will delve a little into the science of kefir.

---

* Anti-tumor agents in kefir have been reported by Kubo, et al., and others. I will discuss the anti-tumor effects of kefir in greater detail later on.

Chapter 2

The Quickening

A Very Symbiotic Affair

Kefir fermentation is made possible by three different lactic acid bacteria plus one lactose-fermenting yeast. There is much confusion about yeasts, yet the truth about yeasts is fairly simple: Yeasts are to microbes what mammals are to animals. They represent a whole group of microorganisms that include harmful and beneficial strains. No one would ever think of a horse as a tiger, yet both are mammals. Yet a lot of people think immediately of candida albicans (the tiger!) when hearing the word yeast. The yeasts that help produce kefir are horses and cows, not tigers and hyenas. We will go into more details on yeasts in general in a later section. For now, simply trust that kefir yeast is a good beast of burden working hard at making our lives easier, more pleasant, and more delectable.

Any yeast capable of fermenting sugars, and lactose is a sugar, will also ferment the monoses (simple sugars) of glucose, fructose and mannose. Yet certain beneficial yeasts have certain preferences for their quickening, their stepping up to more complex formations after the fashion of the corals under the sea. In this, the yeasts in, lets say, the kombucha* mushroom are quite different from those in kefir, or, for that matter, the yeasts used in alcohol fermentation.

The moment we look at food fermentation we are automatically taking a mini course in microbiology—the study of microbial life. The microorganisms that impact on our foods comprise a huge class that includes microbes, various fungi, bacteria and yeasts.

A Feast of Yeast

Let us take a good look at the yeasts to find out what they are and what they can do for us. Yeasts are plant-like life forms that, unlike most plants, lack chlorophyll and therefore cannot metabolize using photosynthesis like other plants.

Yet yeasts are classified as plants because they have to grow on something. Specifically, they are single-cell fungi that reproduce by budding or, less frequently, by fission. There are a few exceptional yeasts that form spores and exhibit semi-sexual reproduction without the distinction of being either male or female. This leads to cross-classifications and goes to show us just how intricate nature is. Nature does not always bend to our categorical desire to keep things tidy and classifiable. Nature, I find, prefers the chaotic.

Yeasts have been man's friend from the days of Adam and Eve. An archaeological dig at Thebes unearthed artifacts from around 2,000 BC, that indicated that yeast was in use in bakeries and breweries. This makes yeast the oldest cultivated plant! Archaeological evidence shows that even the earliest civilizations used alcoholic fermentation, though they may not have known exactly how the fermenting came about.

Only in 1680, after the invention of the magnifying lens made it possible, did Antonie van Leeuwenhoek send descriptions of yeast cells he found in a droplet of beer to the Royal Society in London, England. He called them "animalcules." One hundred and fifty years later, in 1818, yeasts were finally officially recognized as "living vegetative organisms." And in 1837 it was suggested for the first time that yeasts eat sugar and, in metabolizing their victuals, excrete alcohol and carbon dioxide. Well now!

This new view was unacceptable to orthodox science, which held to the belief that it was chemical reactions and not living cell fermentation that were at work. As with many other things it seems, the argument had to be

* Kombucha yeasts help produce a delicious-tasting, health-bestowing tea by growing into the Kombucha mushroom. For full details read *Kombucha Rediscovered!*, a book in which I explore another helpful, healthful yeast in this *Rediscovered!* series.

settled by Pasteur, a trained chemist with a bent for biology. Pasteur found that yeasts were indeed living cells that caused chemical changes by fermentation! He then wrote further studies on wine and beer in the years 1866 and 1867. Pasteur, anticipating things to come a hundred years later,[7] knew that fermentation is a substitute for respiration. Today, medical science finds that this might possibly be a key to understanding and treating cancer cell proliferation. (See Reviving Choked-Off Cells, page 31.)

Yeasts are singularly responsible for creating an entirely new science, now called biochemistry, namely the science of the chemistry of living organisms. Biochemistry got its start in the year 1897 when Hans and Eduard Büchner added cane sugar to a yeast extract for medical purposes. To their surprise, rapid fermentation took place. This discovery led to a series of studies that over time evolved into biochemistry. The very word "yeast" comes from the Greek *zestos*, which means "boiled." This "boiling," of course, refers merely to the bubbling observed in yeast fermentation.

To grow, yeasts, like humans, require oxygen, proper temperature and pH levels, sufficient organic carbon, nitrogen and minerals. Some yeasts even require vitamins and other growth factors as well. And in metabolizing, yeasts excrete, for their own good, some wonderful substances, such as amino acids, oligopeptides and nucleotides, which are for our own good. Lots more good things could be said about yeasts. They are, after all, a world unto themselves. But our interest here is in their ability to enhance our food and drink.

The yeasts that help make kefir include the friendly Torula kefir and Saccharomyces kefir yeast. Several strains of yeasts can be present in kefirs, and other friendly yeasts sometimes present are:

* *Ascosporogenous* yeasts: *Genus Saccharoymyces*: *Sacc. cerevisiae* (also called *Sacc. uvarum*), *Sacc. delbreuckii*, *Sacc. exiguous*, *Sacc. florenti nus*, *Sacc. globosus*, the aforementioned *Sacc. kefir*, *Sacc. unisporus*, and *Saccharomyces spp.*
* Of the yeast genus *Kluyveromyces*: *Kl. bulgaricus*, *Kl. fragilis*, *Kl. marxianus ssp. bulgaricus ssp. marxianus.*
* Of the genus *Torulospora*: *T. delbreuckii.*
* Of the imperfect yeasts, genus *Candida* (again, do not confuse these friendly Candida yeasts with *Candida albicans*! Remember my horse and tiger analogy): *C. kefyr, Candida (Torula) kefir, C. pseudotropicalis var. lactosa, Candida spp.*
* Of the genus *Cryptococcus*: *Cr. kefyr.*
* Of the unclassified genus *Mycotorula*: *My. kefyr, My. lactis, My. lactosa.*

- Of the genus *Torulopsis*: *Tp. holmii*, *Tp. kefyr* and, finally,
- Of the genus *Torula*: *T. kefir*.

There is no doubt that the foremost authorities on kefir in North America are the members of the probiotics team. The term "probiotics" was coined for specially cultured friendly bacteria helpful for restoring total health to the human intestinal tract. According to the inventors of the term, authors Leon Chaitow and Natasha Trenev[8], kefir grains should contain approximately five to ten percent yeasts, which accounts for kefir being slightly alcoholic. The final alcoholic percentage of kefir will differ depending on the percentage of yeast. Modern kefirs tend to have less alcohol (0.2 to 0.5 percent) than the older, traditional kefirs, which had up to three percent alcohol.

In producing kefir, any and all of these yeasts cooperate closely with lactic acid bacteria in a very symbiotic way of mutual benefit. So, let us look a bit closer at the beneficial bacteria that help us to make kefir.

Culturing Lactic Acid Critters

In considering lactic acid bacteria it is necessary to understand the game of cops and robbers. The bacteria are the robbers because they are often implicated in disease. It is somewhat more difficult to understand that while there are many dangerous (unfriendly) bacteria robbers, there are far more useful, harmless or friendly bacteria cops. By way of explanation consider the following: Bacteria share life and reproduction with human beings on this planet of ours. How do we differentiate human beings? Some human beings are our friends and daily helpers, others we find a bit dangerous or downright unfriendly. Now, simply replace human beings with the word bacteria.

Most bacteria reproduce by fission, that is by spontaneous cell division. Some bacteria produce asexual spores for their division. Bacteria are generally distinguished by the shape and form their cells take. Straight or curved and rod-shaped bacteria are called bacilli. Spherical bacteria are called cocci. The cocci are further divided into diplococci (two adhering cells), streptococci (straight chain of cells), staphylococci (sheet of cells) and sarcina (three-dimensional cell pack). There are further subdivisions, but this will suffice for our needs.

One other group of bacteria that deserves mention are the bifidobacteria. The bifidos are the friendly bacteria of the large intestine in adult humans.[9] Their numbers apparently decline with age or chronic conditions. Conversely, it is suggested that chronic conditions are caused by such a bacterial decline in the bowels. This is one of the best reasons I have come across for the need to regularly provide the system with friendly bacteria.

Factors that can cause a sudden decline in bifidos in children include sudden dietary changes, the use of antibiotics, infections, vaccinations and, believe it or not, sudden weather changes. In adults, more drastic events contribute to the loss of bacteria. There are many culprits: steroids; disturbed gastric function; disturbed digestive tract motility (diarrhea, constipation); suffering from altered acidity due to aging; pernicious anemia; diverticulosis; regional enteritis (also called regional ileitis or Crohn's disease); x-rays; other radiation exposure; cirrhosis of the liver; immune deficiencies; any chronic disease state. What to do?

A healthy bifido presence can be supported by consuming a primarily vegetarian diet, as the consumption of much meat tends to depopulate the bifidos. The drinking and eating of all kinds of lactic acid-fermented foods, milk products, vegetables, teas (e.g., kombucha), etc., helps to reestablish the bifidos, and there we are with kefir again and the lactic acid bacteria.

Typically, lactic acid bacteria are both cocci and bacilli. They are of the greatest importance in food fermentation, especially of milk products. They also ferment sauerkraut, kombucha, pickles, sausage, sourdough bread and soda crackers, as well as a number of lactic wines. Lactic acid bacteria are divided into homofermentative and heterofermentative bacteria. While homofermentative lactic acid bacteria produce mainly lactic acid, heterofermentative bacteria produce—besides lactic acid—ethanol, acetic acid, glycerol, mannitol and CO_2 anaerobic from fermentable carbohydrates.

Characteristic*	Homofermentative	Heterofermentative
End product	Mainly lactic acid	Mainly lactic acid, CO_2
Bacilli	Lactobacillus (16 species)	Lactobacillus (11 species)
Cocci	Pediococcus (5)	Leuconostoc (6)
	Streptococcus (21)	

Total number of species: 42   17

The lactic acid bacteria used in kefir are primarily the lactic streptococci. The kefir starter culture specially formulated by Goodlife Company and Friends also shows in laboratory analysis the bacteria Lactobacillus brevis (two

*Source: Buchanan and Gibbons (1974)

strains) and Lactobacillus fermentum as well as the yeast Cryptococcus laurentii. Their formula has been patented in Australia.

According to writer and probiotics researcher Natasha Trenev, over 400 species of bacteria eventually inhabit the digestive tract of a healthy adult human. Many got there through lactic acid fermentation. In total, the many billions of bacteria living in our intestinal world add up to three and one-half pounds (about one and one-half kilos). Not all of these are friendly, of course, but live in a sometimes precarious balance, just like people with each other.

Kefir grains contain microscopic organisms that live together in harmonious symbiosis. The homofermentative and heterofermentative streptococci and the yeasts in kefir grains are particularly sensitive to changes in production method. The resultant quick change in taste and texture makes the commercial production of kefir far more complicated than that of yogurt. This is one more reason why kefir is best made at home.

Part II

FERMENTING FUN

'What does it live on?'
Alice asked, with great curiosity.
'Sap and sawdust,' said the Gnat.

THROUGH THE LOOKING-GLASS
LEWIS CARROLL

Chapter 3

Fun and Fundamentals of Food Ferments

Fascinating Ferments

Most people's diet is devoid of fermented food and drinks other than alcoholic beverages. Few people ever eat lactic acid-fermented foods or drink lactic acid-fermented drinks. This is true even of those who eat commercial yogurt. Though many people eat yogurt, it is most often "pseudo-yogurts" that are consumed and they no longer contain adequate quantities of beneficial cultures, most often because the yogurt is heat-treated, killing off the live ferments. According to researcher Khem Shahani, Ph.D., Professor of Food Sciences and Technology at the University of Nebraska, and a consultant to the industry, centrifugation of commercial products is another treatment that results in insufficient microorganisms (ferments) in the yogurt.

Yet it is the ferments that are the magic key in the realm of nutrition. Ferments are supermetabolizers that cause such miracles as food constituent conversion, nutrient assimilation, cell transformation, elemental transmutations and plant and animal metamorphoses. They help the diseased body reassemble healthy tissues. Ferments are the ultimate promoters of continued good health. But why should this be so? Where does the energy for transmutation come from? Well, you see, ferments are minuscule converter reactors that create tremendous energy for living tissues. Inside our bodies, ferments—or enzymes, as we moderns prefer to call them—control anabolism (synthesis of complex molecules) and catabolism (breakdown of complex molecules). Enzymes are in charge of the build-up and separation of the metabolic pathway. So it behooves us to look a little closer at these magical enzymes.

Enlivening Enzyme Eccentricity

Every modern lock has a unique key. Enzymes are like keys in that they are highly specific in their tasks. Examples of such specific enzymes are the amylases. They catalyze the conversion of starches to sugars. Protease, another enzyme, unlocks the mechanism that reduces proteins. Lipase enables the break-up of fats. Oxidase by its "turning in the lock" prevents oxygen in nutrients from interfering with intestinal nutrient absorption.

Every living cell needs enzyme helpers—ferments!—for mastering the huge task of transmutation in metabolic energy conversions. It is the totality of this act we call metabolism. In discussing enzymatic catalysis, it helps to know that the word enzyme comes to us from the Greek "enzym" and that "enzumos" means "leavened." Leavening involves mixing in something to induce a general change for the better. And as you probably know from experience, leavened bread is quite a different product than unleavened bread.

Just as most breads need leavening, so every human cell needs specific enzymes (leavenings) for the many steps of anabolism and catabolism. A living cell contains thousands of different enzymes whose task it is to hasten or to hinder or to fix living metabolic processes. Without the presence of active enzymes, cell division cannot and does not take place. This means that growth or renewal cannot occur. It also means that substances spotted as injurious, such as harmful bacteria or poisons, cannot be dissolved and eliminated. Without the helping ferments, our cells would be as helpless as we are before a locked car or a locked house or a locked place of work without the key to let us in. Enzymes grant access!

Just as we safeguard our important keys, so our enzymes need protecting. Many enzymes (ferments or leavenings) are sensitive to major fluctuations in temperature (a rise from 78 to 122°F; 25 to 50°C, for example). As a result, they lose their ability to make active, to activate. Suppose the key is rusty and no longer works in the lock. Oil would be needed. Poisons cause similar unwanted effects on enzymes. Many prescription medicines and pharmaceuticals inhibit proper enzyme activity through unwanted side effects. Often enough, the damage to important enzymes can be so overwhelming that a return to normal functioning is no longer possible. The key has broken off in the lock, as it were. You can no longer enter the system even with oil. We must take care to protect these sensitive keys to our system and keep them safe from harm. Holistic nutrition and holistic healing, and fermented milk products, kefir in particular, provide just such a means.

Right Is Right, Left Is Gauche

Kefir contains more L[+] or right-turning lactic acid than D[-] or left-turning lactic acid. The structural formulas of the isomers (chemical substances that have the same molecular formula but different physical and chemical properties due to the different arrangement of the atoms in the molecules) of the two types of lactic acid give a good illustration of how different these two forms really are:

Molecular formulas showing the two isomers of Lactic Acid

O	O
C-OH	C-HO
H-C-OH	HO-C-H
H-C-O	O-C-H
H	H

Left-turning	Right-turning
D[-] Lactic Acid	L[+] Lactic Acid
(levorotatory)	(dextrorotatory)
Turns rays of polarized	Turns rays of polarized
light to the left	light to the right

In the structural formula, O stands for oxygen, H for hydrogen, C for carbon. But notice in particular the arrangement of the OH groups. In the left-turning lactic acid, the grouping is to the right, in the right-turning acid, it is to the left. This is a quirk of science that has led to misunderstandings before. As can clearly be seen, one version is very much like a mirror image of the other. They are indeed very, very similar lactic acids. Yet if we employ the model of lock and key mechanism, we can easily see why only one key fits while the other will not "turn" the lock. Just imagine the formulas above were key bits and you can see how only one could work to unlock a certain lock.

In Germany, manufacturers of soured milk products are already advertising their particular brand as containing mostly right-turning lactic acid, usually 80 percent. Why should they bother? Who cares? Isn't left-turning lactic acid just as good? Besides, have you ever seen anything turning one way or the other? You mean that matters? HOLD IT. Let's examine this directional business and see if it takes us into the right, sorry, proper direction.

After or during vigorous exercise the lactic acid level in the blood rises by five to ten times of normal values. We experience this excess lactic acid as muscle soreness or pain. While this is an unpleasant symptom of lactic acid metabolism, it is balanced by the fact that lactic acid also intensifies our breathing faculties and therefore the oxygen intake into the cells of our brain, liver and kidneys. Right-turning lactic acid is a normal constituent of the human body. It is important, according to scientific experts, that the cells of the heart muscle obtain their energy primarily from right-turning lactic acid.

Right-turning lactic acid is able to increase breathing, that is the intake of oxygen, of highly active cancer cells.[10] Does this mean that cancer cells will proliferate under a diet that includes regular intake of kefir? No. It means that the oxygen-deprived and for this reason proliferating cancer cells are turned in the right direction again!

This is such a complicated mechanism that I have fully delved into it elsewhere. (See Reviving Choked-Off Cells, page 31.) Suffice it here to say that soured milks like kefir, with mainly right-turning lactic acid, represent great value for our health. They increase the metabolism of our tissues, promote intestinal activity and are indispensable cofactors in the prevention and treatment of all malignant conditions.

The Trouble with Left-Turning Lactic Acid

While the individual kinds of soured milks vary considerably in the way they are produced and the use of lactic acid-producing bacteria and ferments, their nutrient and active ingredient content is similar. It is their lactic acid content that is very different. It depends very much on the method employed. An *L. bulgaricus* yogurt, for instance, contains a total of 65 to 70 percent left-turning lactic acid according to one kefir expert. Only the remainder, i.e., up to 30 percent is right-turning.

Consuming left-turning lactic acid can be problematic. On the polarized light circuit at least, being right-turning is far more right than being left-turning. For the human body, only the right-turning, (L+) lactic acid is natural and physiologically correct. Left-turning (D-) lactic acid is a foreign substance for the human organism. It does not contain the necessary enzymes for proper utilization by the body.

The urinary system flushes the majority of left-turning lactic acid out of the system and the liver converts the remainder into carbonic acid and water. For this task the human liver contains a nonspecific enzyme that is not fully functioning in babies. Consequently, babies react to left-turning lactic acid with inner distillation that results in acidosis and increased expulsion through the urine. This causes a disturbance of the mineral household and metabolism. Because of this problem, parents should curtail the consumption of large quantities of lactic acid products by babies. Even so, according to some experts, proper amounts of kefir play a vital role in the development of a healthy digestive tract in babies.

The Food and Agricultural Organization of the United Nations investigated the question of lactic acid fermentation. This resulted in the recommendation that consumption of left-turning lactic acid be limited in adults to 100 mg per/kg of body weight. There is no limitation, however, for right-turning lactic acid for adults. In foods prepared for babies and toddlers, on the other hand, only right-turning lactic acid should be used.

For these reasons, large quantities of yogurt (more than one liter per day), are not good even for adults, as their overwhelming content of left-turning lactic acid can lead to a strain on the metabolism. Consumption of large quantities over extended periods can also harm the flora normally living in the intestines. Homemade, thickened milk on the other hand, contains both kinds of lactic acid, with only a small excess of one kind or the other.

Most kefir contains between 0.85 and 1.5 percent lactic acid. Acidity is a controlling factor in microbiology. A pH (standing for potential hydrogen, i.e., hydrogen potential) below seven is acid, above seven it is alkaline and at seven the pH is neutral. Different cultures require different pH. Final acidity in kefir is below pH 3. As lower pH numbers indicate higher acidity, and higher pH numbers indicate higher alkalinity, kefir is on the acidic side of this scale. The predominant form of lactic acid produced is the right and right-turning form, with some left-turning lactic acid present.

Part III

KEFIR KALEIDOSCOPE

'What did they live on?' said Alice,
who always took a great interest
in questions of eating and drinking.

ALICE'S ADVENTURES IN WONDERLAND
LEWIS CARROLL

Chapter 4

Reviving Choked-Off Cells

Reviving Choked-Off Cells

Kefir has been shown to have anti-cancer and anti-tumor properties. It seems that proliferating cancer cells can be at least partially restored to normal function, i.e., healed through reactivating them to normal function by involving the work of lactic acid in the body. And some of the most respected scientists have suggested a pathway by which lactic acid fermentation might fight mutant cancer cells. To understand this, we must first know that in cancer pathology, the destruction of normal cell respiration is one of the root causes of the disease.*

It helps to understand that if certain processes in the body can go wrong, leading to the proliferation of cells that no longer service the whole body but work against it, then certain other processes may correct the imbalance and restore cellular order. The body's immune system produces T-cells that can destroy tumor cells. Certain chemicals, called carcinogens, can inhibit T-cells by blocking them and effectively locking them out. Now we must find the right key that might unlock the power of the immune system again to successfully deter cancerous growths. There are a number of chemical repressors that successfully fight cancer cells, such as the chemicals employed in chemotherapy. Unfortunately, these chemical agents

* According to cancer researchers Dr. Heinrich Jung, Johannes Kuhl, PhD and others.

31

always produce severe and unwanted side effects. But there is good evidence to support the theory that there is one chemical repressor that fights cancer cells totally without undesirable side effects. That chemical repressor is lactic acid according to Professor Kuhl!

Lactic acid side effects are welcome effects. For instance, during fermentation a slight food decomposition is reversed through the production of new substances. One such substance is acetylcholine, which tones the nerves and improves sleep patterns. B-vitamins are formed as well as various enzymes that assist proper metabolism. The fermentation process also produces choline, which improves, regulates and balances the composition of the blood as well as helps prevent hypertension and the accumulation of unwanted fats. Choline also inhibits sugar formation, making lactic acid-fermented foods safe for diabetics.

Unlike other methods of food preservation (e.g., alcohol, vinegar) lactic acid fermentation continues as a living process and (unlike alcoholic fermentation*) does not kill off the microorganisms doing all the good work. Instead, fermentation introduces useful microorganisms into the system where they work more good in the digestive tract and promote healthy metabolic transmutations.

The growth disturbance that is called cancer results from impaired tissue repair and regeneration processes owing to chronic toxicosis, a cell-destroying factor. The affected cell's ability to breathe—the exchange of carbon dioxide and oxygen—is dangerously inhibited. As a result, the accumulated lactic acid cannot be changed back into carbohydrate (milk sugar, lactose) from which it was made in the first place. It also can no longer be metabolically separated, that is burned into its final constituents.

Healthy cells continually produce carbon dioxide, which then combines with water to form carbonic acid, which in turn dissociates into simpler components. The amount of oxygen needed to metabolize lactic acid accumulated, for instance, during physical exercise, is known as the oxygen debt. This debt must be paid by the cell and requires a working respiratory system. This in turn requires fuel in this case oxygen, for burning. Oxygen is the power source and the raw material for all cell regeneration. So far so good. The trouble with cancerous cells is that they cannot or do not breathe! Instead, they ferment! Healthy lactic acid taken into the body from outside through eating or drinking kefir fosters the healing of such sick cells and aids the body by driving away the noxious acids.

In order to make sense of the seeming contradiction of the ferment of cancer being helped by ferments, it is necessary to look at the work of the

---

* For example, in a herbal tincture like Echinacea, alcohol-soluble substances, e.g., oils, are extracted from the herbs and are concentrated in the tincture. A tincture is therefore not the result of a fermentation process.

German physician and scientist Johannes Kuhl, who has studied the workings of cancerous cells and the healing action of lactic acid. According to Dr. Kuhl, "Cancer is not a localized tumor only, but a generalized ailment of the entire organism." Therefore, to remove part of the body through surgery, or to submit a cancerous organ to gamma radiation is hurtful and insufficient as it does not remove the root cause. Kuhl considers such methods actually harmful as the most immediate effect of surgery and radiation is to further weaken the patient.

"Lactic acid is the functional element of growth in nature and the regenerative component for damaged plant and animal cells," writes Dr. Kuhl in his book *Checkmate to Cancer (Schach dem Krebs)*. He goes on, "It's the lack of the presence of nature-grown lactic acid in our daily diet that is the real problem."

Dr. Kuhl is working from within the framework of isopathic law, which holds that a disease contains the means for its cure in its own causative agent, when he suggests that fermented milk products are invaluable as a preventive and healing agent in disease. According to isopathic law, lactic acid from ferments like kefir removes excess lactic acid from body cells. Therapeutic administrations of lactic acid-fermented foods are therefore curative of body cells that are "fermenting." Following the isopathic law that was first applied by Hippocrates and reaffirmed by Paracelsus, Robert Koch and Pasteur, Dr. Kuhl recommends to start cancer treatment with a weak but frequent dose of lactic acid, which should then be gradually increased.

Says he, "In tumor treatment we must treat the very formation of cell life; respiration and fermentation." It is only possible to treat cell respiration indirectly, so as to avoid destroying or paralyzing the cell. This is best accomplished through the ingestion of lactic acid-fermented foods. Latest scientific findings suggest that it is best to introduce lactic acid-fermented foods from a variety of sources, e.g., kefir, kombucha, lactic acid-fermented fruits, lactic acid-fermented vegetables, etc.

Dr. Kuhl emphasizes that it is "completely meaningless to expect a normal fermentation in an artificial tissue, such as cancer. The over-acidification of the body cells is not to be fought and eliminated allopathically, but isopathically. Nobody can change that. Preventing cancer means, according to the results of my research, seeing to it that there is a regulation of the lactic acid metabolism in the body cells (tissues), so that the physiological (that is the normal quantity needed by the body) lactic acid never becomes a pathologically overabundant substance."

Kuhl goes on to explain that, "the cancer disease is a chronic disturbance of the lactic acid metabolism. . . . The toxic amount of lactic acid present causes precipitous proliferation of cells that do not reach the stage of maturity. This process is called the whip effect. They form the cancer node, or if there is decomposition, the cancer tumor. These immature cells cannot breathe. Since the last cell regeneration has not been reached, they lack a respiratory system."

The body, fighting for survival, wants to regain health. It works to reorganize the affected tissues. It produces a supportive growth substance, lactic acid. But the noxious elements present prevent the sick cells from healing. The body, its system gone awry, produces more lactic acid. The cells must regain their health, that is become mature and then proliferate, to eliminate defective tissue. But when the level of the growth substance (lactic acid) becomes toxic, the cells are driven to multiply but can no longer mature. The byproduct of this cellular struggle is a malignancy. The immature cells fail to develop breathing capacity.

"Cancer," according to Kuhl, "is a chain of causes [and] the only sure way for overcoming cancer is prophylaxis through nutrition which . . . protects the fermentation and hormone systems of the organism from damage, maintains the ability of the lymphatic defense apparatus to function preventatively, and prohibits the forming of diseased lactic acid through cancer poisons."

Kuhl's analysis of the nature of cancer, the destructive nature of the body's endogenous lactic acid, and the role that lactic acid plays constructively, are nothing short of astonishing. Yet the universally held idea of cancer as a localized condition prevails even today in most medical centers, where researchers are still desperately seeking, but not finding, the magic bullet that will cure cancer.

Dr. Kuhl believes that people who eat lactic acid-fermented foods hold the reins of their lives in their own hands. They are preventing malignant tumor growths by observing the isopathic law, even if they do so unknowingly.

Oy Whey, Kefir Cures All

It may be difficult to believe so much of such a simple food as kefir, but soured milks in general have illustrious reputations. In fact, kefir can prevent illnesses and heal many diseases not associated with malignancies.

Kefir establishes and/or reestablishes a healthy intestinal flora, thereby helping many gastrointestinal disorders. Kefir also exhibits bactericidal properties, thus acting as a natural antibiotic that does not build up the negative side effects of today's artificial antibiotics. The whey from cultured milk shows a wide spectrum of antibiotic properties. Studies show that this type of whey neutralizes most pathogenic bacteria within twenty-four hours.[11] Various medical studies confirm kefir's usefulness in the treatment of psoriasis, eczema, allergies, migraine, gout, rheumatic and arthritic conditions, colitis and irritable bowel syndrome.

The World Health Organization (WHO) has reported on the medical use of kefir in the treatment of tuberculosis and typhoid fever. Other reports relate how diarrhea in newborn babies caused by *E. coli* was controlled with fermented milk. The benefits of kefir also extend to the prevention of otitis, pharyngitis and pneumonia in infants. Strangely enough, kefir also works as a laxative. It is an effective but gentle treatment for overcoming constipation. Not surprisingly, fermented milks are helpful for elderly sufferers of chronic constipation. Medical practitioners in Germany and in Russia prescribe kefir for this condition.

Having witnessed the healthful workings of soured milks, the most famous physicians of antiquity, like Galen, prescribed fermented milks like kefir to their patients. Simultaneously, kefir arose as a folk medicine and "secret medicine" among tribal healers and was used to treat dysentery and inflammatory diseases of the stomach, liver and intestines, as well as to increase appetite and improve skin tone.

Other claims (not necessarily confirmed by studies) include the treatment of metabolic disorders such as diabetes and hypertension, atherosclerosis[12] and allergic conditions.[13] Kefir can also help to prevent or heal cystitis, which involves bladder inflammation, urinary tract infection, and possibly the kidneys, the urethra, and, in males, the prostate. Patients put on a kefir diet have overcome anxiety[14] more easily. Kefir consumption mitigates the negative effects of radiation, irradiation and toxic pollutants.[15]

Some researchers suggest that lowered estrogen levels in women are a factor in the onset of osteoporosis.[16] Interestingly, it is also reported that a lack of or low levels of intestinal flora contribute to the lowering of estrogen levels in women years before the onset of menopause. Thus, increasing the intestinal flora may protect women from hormonal imbalance and, consequently, from osteoporosis. So, as you can see, there are many reasons to supplement the diet with kefir.

Babies Benefit Before and After Birth

Especially during pregnancy, mother and baby benefit from milk products. Kefir offers in good moderation and in a superior mix all the natural fat and protein requirements for baby and mom. Milk fat and milk protein, milk calcium (and vitamin D important to calcium absorption) and phosphor are the most easily digested forms of these nutrients. They are vital to healthy growth of babies and safeguard the bones and teeth of expectant or nursing mothers. Lactic acid-fermented milk products allow mothers to pass the goodness of kefir on to the fetus.

The gastrointestinal tract of the fetus is completely sterile and free of any bacterial colonies, good or bad. During birth, in its passage through the birth canal, the baby picks up bacteria that take up residence in the gastrointestinal tract. This process happens so fast that a few days after birth the intestinal tract of babies is colonized by bacteria. Most enter the system through the mouth. Interestingly, it was found that vaginal birth babies colonized quicker than babies born by Cesarean section, confirming the importance of a normal birth procedure if possible. Breast feeding also accelerates the colonization of friendly bacteria in the infant, such as the bifidobacteria.

'I don't believe that pudding ever will be cooked!
And yet it was a very clever pudding to invent.'
'What did you mean it to be made of?' Alice asked.

THROUGH THE LOOKING-GLASS
LEWIS CARROLL

Chapter 5

Making Kefir

Kefir Fervor

We must thank Natasha Trenev, the co-author of *ProBiotics*, for bringing kefir grains to the United States. In her book, Ms. Trenev states that she brought kefir grains from the then USSR into the US in 1960. Her home state of California, however, ruled that cultured milk could not contain yeasts, and so the California kefir is not the traditional kefir of eastern peoples. Other States, and in particular New York, were more tolerant of yeast in cultured milk. However, Ms. Trenev reports that some yeast-based kefir is now for sale in the Pacific Northwest.

Indeed, today North American consumption of all fermented dairy products is on the rise. Statistics confirm the increased consumption of yogurt and buttermilk. Cultured butter*, too, is finding more and more friends, especially as word gets around about how much healthier and more easily digested such butter is compared to the regular North American-styled salted butter.

I predict that consumption of kefir will rise dramatically in the years to come. At first it will seem quite slow, but it will gain momentum. And, similar to the history of yogurt, suddenly everyone will be eating kefir and the next thing we know it will be taken for granted as part of our regular

---

* I shudder every time I preorder and get served with a vegetarian meal on an aircraft a special brand of especially "healthful margarine", so one of these days I must write a book on the healthfulness of cultured butter. Despite all the propaganda, it is still a very good fat to eat! Margarine was invented by the French aristocracy as substitute food for the peasant classes!

diet, as yogurt is now. At that point, commercialism will no doubt have taken over and produced kefir fervor in all of us. We will be in a kefir boom.

You can get the jump on this boom with the help of the information that follows: Everything you need to know to make great-tasting kefir at home. And with Goodlife Company's Kefir Maker it couldn't be easier.

Grains of the Prophet Mohammed

Traditionally, making kefir involved putting milk and the kefir culture (the grains) into a sack made from an animal hide. The sack was left hanging in the sun during the day and brought into the house at night and hung close to the door. Anyone entering or leaving the house was expected to prod the sack to mix its contents. As the kefir was used, more milk was added to keep the fermentation process going.

Traditional lactic kefir cultures come as frozen concentrates. (This is still the way for yogurt makers.) There are two types of kefir cultures, lactic acid fermentation and alcohol/lactic acid fermentation. The alcohol/lactic acid fermentation is the more popular method and considered the traditional one by most. Of course, using the traditional method of making kefir is similar to making Kombucha - a bit complicated and a bit untidy. You will need a thermometer, suitable pots, running water and many kitchen towels around you. The modern version of that traditional method is described below in more detail. The method is a bit messier than the Donovan method using the Goodlife Kefir Maker.

Making Kefir Using the Traditional Method

There are two ways of making kefir: the old traditional and the simple modern method. Let's look at the old way of making kefir first. But if you feel like skipping this section, feel free to go to page 43 for the simplest possible and most modern way of making kefir. Unless you use raw milk from a cow or other milk-producing animal, you do not need to heat, i.e., to sterilize, the milk. Any milk you obtain from a store will work just fine for kefir making without preheating. And, once the kefir grains have been started and the milk is stored at about 22°C for 18 to 24 hours, usually overnight, you'll have the most beautiful kefir. It really is as simple as that. Raw milk (unpasteurized, non-homogenized) contains in excess of 100,000 microorganisms of various kinds, which over the long haul could interfere with the kefir grains. Such milk is generally only available to dairy farmers. At the risk of sounding controversial, however, I would still opt for the raw milk and replace the kefir grains as necessary if they become too small or turn yellowish over time. The problem is, you can't usually buy such milk unless you live on a farm or in California (see reference to certified raw milk on page 12).

1. It is best to transfer the milk for your kefir to a suitable preserving jar that is equipped with a rubber ring. Pour in the milk so as to leave at least a 1-inch (3-cm) clearance at the rim. To avoid contamination, seal the jar and let the milk cool to 70°F (22 to 25°C).

   Note A: The clearance will be needed as the fermentation process causes slight pressure build-up caused by the creation of carbon dioxide.

   Note B: Though tolerant of temperature variation, fluctuation of temperature does affect the performance of yeast and will affect the fermented product.

2. Place 1/2 to 1 cup of kefir grains (see reference section for obtaining grains) into the milk. According to the orthodox method, the more grains you add, the thicker the finished product will be and the faster it will ferment. Cover the "kefired" milk tightly by sealing the jar.

   Note: Sealing the jar will still leave enough oxygen in the mix for the yeast cells in kefir to perform unimpeded.

3. Incubate for 24 to 36 hours at 70°F (21°C), or for two or three days at 50°F (10°C). Shaking the glass now and then will increase the formation of carbon dioxide and smoothen the coagulation process, making for a finer distribution throughout the milk and creating a smoother kefir. This method will produce 0.8 percent acidity, 1 percent ethanol and an amount of carbon dioxide (CO_2), depending on how often the mixture is shaken. If you find that the culture sets too fast or becomes too thick, you have added too many grains to the milk.

   Note A: The kefir grains will first sink to the bottom but will soon begin to rise and finally float on top of the milk. This rising confirms that fermentation is taking place. Some of the bubbles will not rise fully but stay on in pockets of the slowly solidifying milk.

   Note B: Shorter fermenting time (24 hours) makes the final kefir sweeter; longer fermenting (36 to 48 hours) will increase souring. Vary according to taste preference. This may take some experimenting until you get the hang of it.

Note C: Temperature variations influence the result in a similar way, with higher temperatures increasing souring (due to increased bacterial activity) and lower temperatures yielding a milder kefir.

Note D: The amount of kefir grains used will again influence the result, with more grains added yielding a greater souring and less grains a milder souring of the kefir. The three methods for variation described in B, C and D may, of course, be combined for fine-tuning your kefir product.

4. If all was done right, on opening the jar a definite popping will audibly-bly confirm that successful carbon dioxide formation took place. You now have a foaming and very refreshing kefir drink before you.

5. Now lift out the grains with a clean spoon and place them in a sieve and rinse them briefly but thoroughly under cold running water, or pour the solution through a sieve into a waiting container, thereby leaving the kefir grains behind in the sieve for rinsing under cold water.

6. Clean the jar that was used for fermenting. Then use again by placing the cleansed kefir grains into a new batch of milk to repeat the process.

7. The grains will multiply, usually doubling in volume within four weeks, so that soon there will be more kefir grains than needed. You may separate them using scissors or a knife or just your clean fingers.

Note: Store surplus grains for making future batches by either freezing or drying them. Dry them in cheesecloth at room temperature for 36 to 48 hours, then store in the refrigerator or freezer. Grains so treated stay active for more than a year.

8. The finished kefir (separated from the grains) will keep in the refrigerator at about 40°F (4°C) for up to two weeks.

If this seems like a lot of fuss and muss you'll be happy to know that there is a new method for making kefir. It's time to meet John Donovan, the inventor of a simple pocket-sized device for successfully making kefir at home without fuss.

*Of course, the first thing to do
was to make a grand survey of the country
she was going to travel through.
'It's something very like learning geography,' thought Alice.*

THROUGH THE LOOKING-GLASS
LEWIS CARROLL

Chapter 6

A Kefir Server – A World Savior

The Goodlife Vision

It is said that John Donovan was "the boy no other child wanted to swap lunches with." His mother's sandwiches were just too wholesome! John Donovan was born in New Zealand in 1954 into a family dedicated to natural living long before it became trendy. John's mother was greatly interested in promoting the key elements of natural health: proper nutrition, positive mind set and proper spirituality.

Some forty years ago, John's mother, Phyllis, was given a kefir culture for fermenting milk, to which the family attributes their outstanding good health and longevity. Young John was fascinated with this culture, and even as a boy dreamed of passing this secret on to the world. He experimented with kefir making endlessly and began thinking of how he could make the kefir grains more widely available.

In April 1992, John founded the Goodlife Company. Starting with only a handful of kefir grains, the Donovans expanded business as they grew more kefir. Then John Donovan designed and patented a simple device for making kefir—the Kefir Maker, a flow-through cone that floats on milk. His initial kefir product was a success. As a result, in 1995 the company moved into larger premises and began exploring international markets.

41

John Donovan and the Goodlife vision have created timely and modern advances in formulating soaps and skin care creams from kefir. John Donovan's ideas and the Goodlife Company's products reflect their mission statement: "To provide opportunities, services and products which empower and enable individuals to take responsibility for their own wellbeing and the wellbeing of the planet." By making kefir at home, you can contribute in a similar way.

With the Goodlife Company Kefir Maker, the grains are easily recovered after use by simply removing the flow-through cone. The kefir culture is a mixture of friendly bacteria and yeasts contained in grains in a small envelope. The small, flexible kefir granules are grown naturally in Australia and consist entirely of 100 percent kefir culture and contains absolutely no fillers.

If you already have a Goodlife Kefir Maker kit you are practically ready to roll. The Kefir Maker comes in a plastic shipping container with a tamperproof seal and screw top. Make sure that the seal is unbroken before opening the Kefir Maker for the first time. Inside you will find:

- 1 envelope containing kefir grains
- 1 kefir grain flow-through cone
- 1 cone lid
- 1 flotation top cover

As I have emphasized, kefir making involves living microorganisms; cleanliness is therefore important. So please be sure to wash your hands before handling the grains, the cone and the top. Make sure all containers, spoons and anything else you may be using are clean. You are ready for processing as now comes the modern and simple way of making kefir. The quickest and best way to describe it is so very simple that something seems missing. It really is just a 1,2,3:

1. Pour milk into the plastic container
2. Drop in the Kefir Maker cone
3. Let stand at room temperature for 24 hours. Enjoy!

Not nearly complicated enough? Well, let's have all the details of the above method:

Making Kefir with the Goodlife Kefir Maker

Note: The shipping container should be used only to make the first two batches, which are required to "waken-up" the kefir grains. But, the kefir from these batches needs to be thrown out as it does not taste good as yet.

1. Open the envelope which contains the kefir starter culture or grains.

2. Tip the kefir grains into the open cone.

3. Clip the small lid onto the top of the cone to lock in the grains.

4. Snap the cone into the flotation top.

5. Fill the container with 1 to 2 liters of milk to within 1/2 inch from top. Either way though, it is best to start your kefir batch with whole milk or standard milk. All milks, even soy milk, will work, with the exception of rice milk. After you have successfully completed your kefir, try for a creamier consistency with your next batch by using half-and-half or whipping cream.

6. Place the flotation cone into the container or glass jar. According to John Donovan, you will get the best results using a ceramic pot with a lid. It will float on top of the milk.

7. Place the container or jar in a warm place away from direct sunlight. Fermenting temperature is 72 to 78°F (21 to 26°C). The temperature on top of the refrigerator in moderate climates is around 78°F (26°C), which is ideal.

8. Open after 24 hours. You will have now a soft food, the consistency of clubberd milk, that you can eat with a spoon, either at room temperature or chilled after refrigerating. If you stir kefir, you can drink it and it tastes like buttermilk. (See Part IV – A Whirl of Recipes)

9. Remove the kefir cone.

10. Rinse the cone with small lid still on under lukewarm running water. Do not remove the small lid from the cone! Instead, swish the cone vigorously under the tap and leave as is. Tap off excess water.

11. Snap flotation top back on cone and store in plastic container.

Simply repeat the 1, 2, 3 basic method (i.e., detailed steps 1 through 11) for a continuous supply of fresh kefir. Or you can store the ready-to-go Kefir Maker in the fridge. When you want another batch of kefir simply take out the jar, repeat the process and place on top of the fridge and you are automatically back to fermenting. Be sure to replace the milk weekly if storing longer.

For safety reasons, it is better to use a plastic container when taking your Kefir Maker on vacation or business trips. No matter what container you use, always make sure it comes with a lid that can be tightly sealed. Remember, the less the fermenting milk is exposed to the air (oxygen), the better the kefir will turn out.

Once started, the Kefir Maker will, on average, turn 1 – 2 liters of milk into kefir every 24 to 36 hours at a temperature of 72 to 78°F (21 to 26°C).

What Could Go Wrong?

As we all know, Murphy is always diligent. Even foolproof things can go wrong. Yet in a worst case scenario, there are still only seven things that could go wrong in modern kefir making and they can be easily itemized thus:

1. The milk or cream that you have been using could have been too old!

2. The container used (glass, ceramic or plastic) was not sterile!

3. The container used was made of metal, (aluminum, iron or stainless steel)! Or an enamel container used was chipped. (Glass is best!)

4. Temperature was too cold: At below 21°C, fermentation will proceed too slowly or not at all.

5. Temperature was too hot: Too hot and fermentation proceeds too fast. The milk solids separate too soon and before being properly soured. No need to panic though—just strain the fermentation through cheese cloth and you will have the nicest bread spread—just not what kefir is supposed to be. Compare the result to kefir cheese (see paragraph on cheese making).

6. Kept too long in fermentation. Results are as in 5 above, but now soured (see cheese making).

7. RIP—The culture died! Maybe it wasn't properly nourished. Maybe it "fell asleep" or was kept in the cold for too long . (Incidentally, if you don't want to make kefir for a while—let's say you're going on a holiday—just add fresh milk to the kefir maker and store in the fridge. Your kefir will stay active forever.)

8. Should your kefir have "fallen asleep," simply start it again with "Waking the Sleeper" as described on page 46.

9. If all else fails, you can simply ask your supplier for a new kefir starter. They will replace the bacteria part of the Kefir Maker.

Storing Your Kefir Maker

When not in use, you can simply store your Kefir Maker in the fridge after rinsing the grains clean. It is easiest to keep the cone containing the grains in the shipping container or in a glass jar filled with fresh milk. Fully submerge the cone and seal the container or jar. Every week, or at least every other week, replace the milk with fresh milk. Then, if you want to make a fresh batch of kefir, take the cone with the grains out of the storage container and float on top of fresh milk, any quantity up to 2 liters.

If you are going to be absent for longer than two weeks and have no one to take care of your Kefir Maker, you may do one of two things:

1. Rinse and drain the kefir grains as usual, then place in the shipping container or jar and seal tightly so that no air can escape. You can use hot wax to complete the seal. Store in freezer until needed again.

2. Rinse, drain and air-dry the kefir grains in the cone using a fan or by placing in a room with good air circulation. Once dry, seal in the shipping container or jar and store in a dry, cool, dark place. Stored by either method they should be good for up to two years.

When not in use, simply store unit in milk in the fridge. Every week replace with fresh milk. If you are going to be absent: Rinse and place cone in shipping container. Store in the freezer. To reactivate the grains in the cone, place in milk and process normally. Remember to throw out your first two kefir batches after the kefir grains have not been in use.

With the Goodlife Company Kefir Maker, local resources and our own dishes, we can achieve a tremendous cutback in waste: environmental waste, energy waste and resources waste. The net result will be a greener earth, a cleaner planet to live on and less pollution of our air, water and soil. Such self-reliance will not only help you be healthier but will also help create a better environment for all of us sharing this planet.

In Canada and the United States, the in-home Kefir Maker can be obtained, as I understand it, for under $25.00 from:

Teldon of Canada Ltd.
7436 Fraser Park Drive
Burnaby BC V5J 5B9
800-663-2212
604-436-0545
Fax: 604-435-4888

The folks at Teldon would also be happy to refer you to a store in your hometown where you can purchase the Kefir Maker, and, of course, provide you with Kefir Maker replacement grains, should yours ever die.

Waking the Sleeper

When you use your new Kefir Maker for the first time, you are literally waking it from a long sleep. As a result, the first few times you make kefir it may take a bit longer to "set" the milk. It is not unusual to find that your Kefir Maker produces ever better tasting kefir as time goes by.

The culture is quite small in the beginning, but will eventually grow into larger granules. When cleaning the cone, be careful not to accidentally flush the culture down the drain. It is best not to open the cone for at least six to eight weeks. In that time period the culture will have grown substantially.

If you need to open the cone thereafter, be careful not to damage it. Carefully insert a pointed object into one of the slits and gently twist. After removing the grains to a safe place (such as a fine sieve), wash the cone, its snap-on lid and the circular top with soap and hot water to rid of all contaminants. Rinse the grains in the sieve under warm water, then put them back in the cone and replace the lid.

In time, your cone may no longer be large enough to contain the growing culture. Never let the cone be more than half full with culture. Excess culture needs to be transferred to another cone. Chances are that by the time that happens you and your family will be so taken with kefir you will want to have a second cone. At that point, you can always buy another Kefir Maker to obtain an extra cone. As of this writing at least, you cannot buy just a replacement cone.

An Authentic Udder Cola

Kefir, and in true milk drinks only kefir, can be made to offer true fizz and pop and tingle. For a great tongue tingling, you turn your kefir into milky champagne. How? Simply let it ferment again, this time inside a bottle. To obtain true milk champagne, vigorously shake the kefir being fermented now and then during the first 24-hour period. After 24 hours, separate the kefir from the grains in the previously prescribed manner. You now have a kefir with about 0.2 percent alcohol, containing only a little carbon dioxide. Now put this kefir into a clean champagne bottle, filling it to one-third. Then fill the bottle to within two inches (5 cm) of the rim with the same kind of milk used for the initial fermenting. Finally, cork the bottle and shake it every hour.

Despite the grain removal, fermentation continues on the strength of the remaining microorganisms. After some 60 hours of this, shaking it as often as possible at least during the day, you will have a strong champagne kefir waiting for you in the bottle. Uncorking the bottle will give the same surprising pop that regular bubbly gives! The emerging creamy drink now contains a lot of carbon dioxide. There are many connoisseurs of kefir champagne. Some of them even go so far as to ferment the bottled kefir under a cooler temperature of around 55°F (12°C). This slows down the fermentation process and produces an especially tasty and highly valued variety of kefir champagne.

Nulla fit sine caseo bona digestio
SCHOOL OF SALERNO, 12TH CENTURY

Making Kefir Cheese

The very best cheese you will ever have tasted, and a great new taste treat for any cheese lover will be kefir cheese! The protein and the milk fat in kefir are all the basic ingredients needed for making delectable kefir cheese. No need to be concerned about too much fat. The total fat content of finished kefir will be approximately 1.5 percent. Most of the remaining fat will have been metabolized during fermentation. Combining different milks, such as standard, whole, skim, buttermilk, and using milk from different animals (cow, goat, sheep, horse, etc.) and some additional ingredients, can result in hundreds of different kefir cheeses! If you are knowledgeable in cheese making, other microorganisms may be added, depending on the desired end product.

For kefir cheese production, use finished lactic acid-fermented kefir. Make sure it was made with the freshest milk possible. The fresher the milk, the better the resulting cheese will be. Also make sure that the grains have been removed. This will be easiest if you have used the Goodlife Company Kefir Maker.

To make kefir cheese:

1. Make kefir with whole milk, half-and-half or standard milk with 20 percent whipping cream.

2. Place in a warm spot.

3. Ferment for 24 to 48 hours. (Double the normal fermenting time.) Ferment until milk solids appear.

4. In the final stage of fermenting, place container in an extra warm spot for 2 to 3 hours. (Either the top of the fridge or in the oven with the pilot light on.)

5. Remove and pour through a cheesecloth. Let stand for 24 to 48 hours or until kefir cheese is harder than sour cream, but not as hard as cream cheese.

6. Enjoy delicious kefir cheese in a variety of recipes.

You do not need to throw away the whey. It is wholesome and can be drunk as is, or you may add it to other food recipes or use it in soup stocks. If you have no immediate plans for it, simply pour it into a glass jar, and with lid on, store in the fridge for up to five days. Remember that kefir whey is very similar to buttermilk and is therefore an excellent thirst quencher. Remember, though, to discard any unused kefir after five days. Kefir, like any good food, does not last indefinitely even in your fridge. And it is always good to err on the side of safety, so "when in doubt, throw it out!"

The remaining curds are your new kefir cheese! It will be thick with big curds. Enjoy as is or use with fruit or vegetables. Of course, the kefir cheese can now be flavored with other cheeses or in other ways. Adding a little Parmesan or any of the blue cheeses will give you a different taste experience. You may wish to add some herbs or spices. There is practically no limit if you let your imagination run wild.

Remember, while kefir cheese is a wonderful food and remarkably safe, I would always stress that cleanliness is next to godliness when making kefir cheese, even though the occurrence of food poisoning microbes is highly unlikely, given the quality of today's milk products. Moreover, the use of lactic acid bacteria contributes to food safety. Lactic acid bacteria inhibit or even inactivates the growth of toxic bacteria. Tests carried out in 1972 by Gilliland and Speck showed almost complete inhibition of toxic agents by lactic acid bacteria. It follows then, that kefir cheese is safer than cheeses made without lactic acid fermentation.

Finally, it is worth noting that the flavor of the cheese will vary with your location, altitude and climate. This accounts for the great variety of cheeses in the world, and explains why, for instance, Swiss cheese made outside Switzerland will never taste like Swiss cheese! Of course, in your particular spot in the world, you might easily end up producing a cheese superior to any known. So, give it a whirl and my heartfelt wishes will be with you all the way.

Yours Silkily

Our face and our skin mirror our lifestyle and reflect how well we are inside. The skin—our largest organ—does much more than contain and protect our body from the outside world. It is our organ of physical touch. It maintains a constant reciprocal relationship with the environment. It lives. It breathes. It reacts to stimuli from within and without. And it wants to be babied as much as possible.

Improving skin care is vital when toxic effects damage our skin. Skin conditions, whether caused by accidents, allergies or nervous and metabolic disorders, need tender, loving healing. It also helps to favor cotton, silk, linen, wool, leather, etc., over rayon and other synthetics that curtail the skin's ability to breathe freely. And to avoid possible allergic reactions, wash laundry using modern methods (like laundry disks) or with detergents containing no chemicals.

According to the world's foremost herbal medicine authority, Dr. Rudolf Fritz Weiss, the skin benefits not only from external but also from internal therapeutic agents. The skin has the ability (denied by some medical authorities) to slowly absorb nutrients applied to it and transfer them to the subcutaneous and collagen tissues underneath. This means that the skin will also absorb toxic substances from, for example, sprays, sun lotions and some skin care products. Consequently, it pays to know what is in your beauty products, and one way you can be sure of the ingredients is by making your own.

So, now that you have discovered what a great drink and wonderful food kefir is, I have more great news for you. Kefir makes for some of the best skin products in the world. You can turn your leftover kefir into a skin cleanser and beautifying cream. You practically have your skin care cream in your hands! Milk's gentle cleansing action, remarkable healing quality and valued beauty effect on the skin has been treasured since antiquity. Who has not heard of the rulers of ancient lands bathing in milk? Essential unsaturated fatty acids are the secret skin care ingredient in milk.

The latest discovery in the skin care industry is alpha hydroxy acid (AHA). These fruit acids are found as citric acid in citrus fruit, tartaric acid in grapes, malic acid in apples, and—you guessed it—in kefir, alpha hydroxy acid is in the form of lactic acid.

Fruit acids naturally harmonize with the slight acidity of our skin and hair. Lactic acid creams, by dissolving the lipids that hold old skin cells together, help to remove dead skin particles so that the new skin can emerge into new radiance. This is particularly true if such a cream is used on a regular basis. Other miracles that alpha hydroxy can reportedly perform include reducing the appearance of wrinkles and scar tissue, and fading age spots and freckles (pigmentation from sun exposure).

Given all these great skin care effects, it is hardly surprising that AHA's are so very expensive. Just visit the cosmetics counters of any large department store and you will see what I mean. But now you have AHA as close as your fridge! Kefir contains all the good AHA without any of the negative artificial colorants, dyes, synthetic perfumes, detergents or other strange ingredients that cause people to have allergic reactions to commercial skin care products. If you have particularly sensitive skin, you may wish to carry out a skin patch test with kefir cream. Put a dab on an area of skin and leave for twelve hours. If no reaction occurs, it is safe for you to use.

The Seven Kefir Beauties

Here are the basic recipes for making kefir skin care products:

1. Cleanser

Place 2 tsp. of dried elder flower, or 1 elder flower tea bag, in a cup of boiling water and steep for five minutes. Strain. Add 2 1/2 Tbsp. of liquid honey and allow the mixture to cool to room temperature. Add kefir to the cooled mixture and whip for several minutes until a smooth cream forms.

To use, apply generously over face and neck and clean off with damp cotton swab. Suits all skin types.

2. Facial Scrub

Mix 3 Tbsp. ground almonds with 1/3 cup kefir. Apply and leave on for 1/4 hour. Gently wash off with warm water. This is excellent for exfoliating face and body. Suitable for sensitive skin.

3. Facial Mask

Take 1/2 cup uncooked oatmeal, 3/4 cup kefir and 2 Tbsp. warm liquid honey. Mix kefir and oatmeal and refrigerate for ten hours. Strain, keeping the liquid and discarding the oatmeal. Add the honey and mix well. Apply the mask and leave on for twenty minutes. Rinse well and apply a moisturizer to the face. This is a great mask for oily skin.

4. Moisturizer

Add three flower heads of marigold to one cup of boiling water. Allow to cool, then remove flower heads. Combine marigold liquid with 2 tsp. kefir, 2 tsp. apricot oil, 1/2 tsp. almond oil and 2 Tbsp. thick cream and mix well. Rub into skin until well absorbed. This makes a good day or night lotion for balancing the skin's acid mantle.

5. Hand Cream

Mix 1 Tbsp. almond oil and 1 cup kefir and massage into hands at bedtime. Wear cotton gloves overnight to protect linen. Wash off in the morning. This is a great once-a-week treat.

6. Kefir Bath

Mix 2 Tbsp. melted butter with 2 Tbsp. olive oil and let sit for one hour. Mix in 1 tsp. apple cider vinegar, 2 Tbsp. witch hazel, juice from three apricots (use blender) and 1/2 cup kefir. Stir well. Add 2 beaten eggs and 2/3 cup milk and put through blender. After blending thoroughly add the rest of the milk. This is enough for 6 baths as only a cupful is needed for each bath. You can keep this mix in a sealed bottle in the fridge.

7. Kefir Hair Conditioner

Beat 1 egg yolk. Add 1/2 cup kefir. Mix in 2 tsp. grated lemon rind and 1/2 tsp. kelp powder. Massage this mixture into the hair and scalp and leave on for 30 minutes. Rinse and shampoo normally, but add a little bit of lemon juice to the rinse water.

A Kefir World – A Safer World!

Not so long ago I was touring the supermarkets of Vancouver, British Columbia, in the company of Dr. Hal A. Huggins, an environmentalist dentist seeking to abolish the use of amalgam in dentistry. I was writing *Eliminating Poison in Your Mouth* at the time. Huggins was telling me of the riots in Los Angeles during which an enraged populace ransacked the local supermarkets. While they took away all they could, they never took any of the products stored on the outer walls of the supermarkets, that is, the fresh produce, the vegetables, the fruit, etc. "I would have no trouble shopping in those ransacked stores," he said. Then he added, "I never ever go down the aisles. They only contain dead food in cans, jars and bottles. All I need is right here along the outer wall."

Besides being a comment on our eating habits, Dr. Huggins words illustrate another problem: if most people are shopping in those aisles full of cans, jars and bottles, then most people are contributing terribly to our throw-away society. But we have the power to change that. By paying attention to what we eat and drink, we can have a more positive impact on our world. By making our own yogurt or kefir, we all at once eliminate the need for a large number of plastic containers. Over time, that adds up to thousands of throw-away containers. So, making our own kefir not only gives us a great tasting drink and food, it also makes us "greener." We are actively participating in cleaning up our environment.

Think about it. Every day, billions of people eat fermented milk products like yogurt and kefir. Does it make sense to buy these foods in containers when we can simply and more easily make them at home? We will not have to wait long to find out if kefir is indeed the twenty-first century yogurt. By all accounts it will be. A natural food that can heal and do all the beneficial things kefir does should outshine and outlive any of the fashionable drugs that are continuously presented to the public.

At this writing, the latest craze is synthetic melatonin. In its natural form, melatonin is a pigmentation hormone released by the pituitary gland. In its synthetic form it promises longevity. In Canada it is still prohibited because of possible side effects and a lack of believable studies. If you are like me, inclined toward the natural, do yourself a "flavor" and make your own soured milk at home. You will never go thirsty, never go hungry and never get sick—not in a thousand years.

Live long and prosper!

> *"all sorts of things,' said the Sheep: 'plenty of choice,*
> *only make up your mind. Now, what do you want to buy?'*
> *'To buy!' Alice echoed in a tone that was half astonished*
> *and half frightened – ...'I should like to buy a kefir,*
> *please,' she said timidly. How do you sell them?'"*

ADAPTED FROM THROUGH THE LOOKING-GLASS
LEWIS CARROLL

Chapter 7

Kefir – A New Industry

Kefir of Kiev

"Believe it," Mike Smolyansky says, "in Russia it's a must! All babies at the age of six months are introduced to kefir, and rightly so, as it is the world's most delicious food." Then he corrects himself with a smile, "really, I should have said 'Ukraine' because I'm from Kiev." Mike tells me that kefir became his vision after he learned of its healthfulness from a Russian compatriot, the 1908 Nobel prize laureate and kefir researcher, Elie Metchnikoff. The professor discovered that kefir activates saliva flow and other digestive juices, stimulates peristalsis and restores intestinal flora, all of which makes it a choice food.

Mike relates how in 1976 at age 29 he left the city of his birth. After many adventures, Mike Smolyansky settled in Chicago, the city of his American dream. Here, Mike made his kefir available to all. To set himself up, he obtained a master's degree in engineering, then another in food processing. Mike was making kefir available, first to Americans, then to the world.

The Gift of Lifeway

Ten years after his arrival, in 1986, Mike made the giant leap. He founded the Lifeway Company (now Lifeway Food, Inc.) for commercially producing and marketing fermented milk products. A new industry was born. Its aim was to develop specialty dairy foods for health-conscious consumers. Of course, the company's main product is kefir. The Lifeway Company (see Useful Addresses) makes only REAL kefir, using a unique microbial composition that, the company claims, makes it the only real kefir in the USA, and recently in Canada. The cultures used by Mike and Lifeway are:

- *Streptococcus lactis*, which produces L (+) lactic acid in quantity and partly hydrolyses milk proteins; increases digestibility of milk; improves stomach digestion; inhibits harmful microorganisms; produces bacteriolysins.

- *Lactobacillus plantarum*, which is antagonistic to Listeria monocytogenes; produces plantaricin, a bacteriocin inhibiting microorganisms that cause spoilage; is a strong producer of lactic acid; tolerates high concentrations of bile salts; adheres to intestinal mucosa.

- *Streptococcus cremoris*, which has the same properties as *S. lactis*, but is more resistant to phages and increases the flavor of kefir.

- *Lactobacillus casei*, which produces L (+) lactic acid in large quantities; colonizes intestinal tract; adheres to intestinal mucosa; creates favorable environment for microbial homeostasis, limits putrefaction, thus controlling production of toxins; inhibits pathogenic bacteria and prevents diseases due to intestinal infections; limits lactose intolerance; contributes to immunity.

- *Streptococcus diacetylactis*, which has properties identical to *S. lactis*; produces diacetyl, a characteristic aroma of kefir, and CO_2.

- *Saccharomyces florentinus* and *Leuconostoc cremoris*.

The Lifeway people are particularly proud that they were instrumental in getting real kefir accepted and passed by the nutrition authority in the highly regulatory State of New York. This underwrites kefir and contrasts with dairy product sold by other producers and in other states under the name of kefir.

One company, for instance, Alta Dena Certified Dairy of City of Industry in California, produces and markets a 'Kefir Cheese.' I have eaten and liked it. It is a very great tasting and good cheese, but is it kefir?

Advertised as a tangy alternative to sour cream, Alta Dena's Kefir Cheese lists the following fermenting cultures: *L. caucasicus, L. bulgaricus, S. thermophilus* and *L. acidophilus*. Ergo, as Mike of Lifeway is quick to point out, it is a yogurt product and not a true—or as Lifeway puts it, REAL—kefir cheese. Mike bemoans the rather loose standards in some of the States and wishes that they would insist on clearly differentiating between yogurt and kefir culture products. It seems that this section of the act controlling the dairy markets needs restructuring.

Mike and Lifeway say that their kefir products contain all the necessary nutrients (proteins, minerals and vitamins) for the body. Unlike most natural medicines manufacturers, Lifeway recommends most of its kefirs also for consumption by children, expectant mothers (who have trouble finding suitable foods), convalescents, people on sulfonamides or antibiotics for restoring their intestinal flora, and for sedentary persons, who need easily digestible foods. It is noteworthy that in Germany and in many regions of the Far East, kefir is used to treat chronic constipation, often afflicting sedentary people.

Mike got more excited yet about kefir when he found that a noted Danish bacteriologist, Dr. Orla-Jenson, proclaimed that kefir can digest yeast cells and thus exert a reducing and healing effect on Candida, the dreaded yeast infection, in which the highly specific disease-causing *Candida albicans* yeast cells excessively increase in the body*. Kefir also reduces the undesirable cholesterol content in blood. It stimulates the excretion of pancreatic enzymes. This is especially crucial for those in danger of diabetes. The company recommends its kefirs also as the milk of choice for people who normally cannot digest milk sugar. The transformation of milk sugar (lactose) to lactic acid makes digestion of lactose possible for those with lactose intolerance. Finally, Lifeway proclaims that eating kefir increases resistance to colds.

A Public Offering

Following the initial successes, Mike Smolyansky noticed that to grow to its full potential the company needed more capital. The banks were reluctant to give a lot more operating capital to a food company with a product that was all Greek to them.

Then Mike and friends hit on a great idea. Why not make a public offering? Let's go public, Mike declared. Thus, in 1988, Lifeway became a

---

* Other scientific sources of kefir information for which Lifeway expressly acknowledges gratitude and indebtedness include: Dr. Steven Novil, PhD, Dr. N.S. Koroleva, and The International Dairy Federation of Russia, Professor Manfred Kroger, and The Pennsylvania State University.

public company. Soon after, Lifeway Food, Inc. traded on the Nasdaq stock exchange. For the financial year of 1997 – 1998, the company forecasts a 25 – 30 percent increase in revenues while overhead is by now relatively fixed. The years 1992 through 1996 had seen steady and reassuring growth in all sectors of the company's affairs. A substantial increase in the return on equity is forecast for 1997. Return on investment was reported at 19.3 percent in 1996, markedly ahead of many forms of investment returns, especially interest rates.

Fabulous Farmers' Foods

According to Mike Smolyansky, Lifeway is the only maker of 100% fat free real kefir. "The world's first and only fat free commercial kefir," he proudly says. And so Lifeway's flyers announce, "Improving daily life for over 2000 years," in obvious reference to the age-old real traditional kefir food and method the firm employs rigorously.

Their liquid and semi-solid kefirs come in 32-ounce bottles, just about one liter, and today Lifeway makes many types of plain and flavored kefir drinks. The low fat kefirs, which only contain 5 grams of fat per 8 ounce (1/4 liter) serving, contain no saturated fat and are low in cholesterol and sodium, are healthful new additions to their standard kefirs. Yet, the body does need fats, especially the good butterfat, the most easily digested fat for humans! Lifeway gave way to public pressure who is looking for fat-free products, the latest craze hitting North America. Fat free dairy products really do not make sense because the fat carries the vitamin A, which is required for the metabolism and absorption of calcium. I have a hunch that at least where dairy products are concerned this is a passing fad and that we will soon be back to standard milk products with regular fat content.

Personally, I prefer the regular fat kefirs because of the richer taste that is bestowed by the fats. I rationalize this by realizing that lactic acid-fermented milk fats are far more easily digestible than would otherwise be the case. So, take your pick of the many liquid kefirs with various fat contents.

Mike shows me tasty cheeses that are commercially available. Kefir cheese is also known as 'pot cheese' or 'farmers' cheese'. The low fat and fat free kefir drinks the company sells, boast many interesting flavors. Strawberry, banana, cherry, raspberry, peach, and blueberry flavors are offered in addition to plain kefirs of differing fat contents. Real connoisseurs relish the vanilla, chocolate, and Cappuccino kefirs. Lifeway's latest kefir cheese offering is called ELITA (like in *elite*), a fitting label for a real low fat kefir alternative to cream cheese. It's perfect for many modern dishes, as it is appetizing, tasty, delicate, creamy and spreadable. It also makes a great filling for pastries and deserts.

Lifeway's new cultured Farmer Cheese is made according to an old European recipe based on slow draining of the cheese. The Farmer Cheese is commercially available as 'regular', 'low fat', 'fat free' 'pressed,' or as a 'Sweet Mixture' with golden raisins. After testing and tasting most of the Lifeway products, I vouchsafe from personal taste trials that all of their kefir products are outstanding. All enjoy terrific taste—just like grandma made it.

Ingesting and Investing – Healthiest of Food and Fortune

Are you one of those idealists who is interested in not only ingesting the good kefir drinks and cheeses, but also investing in kefir? You can easily help spread (pun intended) the good kefir across the world of natural lifestyles by—but only if you can truly afford to—investing in the world's only publicly traded kefir stock. If your finances allow you trading, why not invest directly or, even better, via a tax shelter such as an RRSP, in the only real kefir stock. Its ticker symbol is LWAY. Its history looks good. Check it out on the internet or call your broker.

The Future of Kefir
Nutritional and Dietary Therapies

Lifeway is feverishly working on a kefir diet based on scientific information. A nutritional professor from Russia is developing choice flavors for a new way of eating and enjoying kefirs. In an about turn, as of 1995, Lifeway is even exporting to Russia. Three years ago, the company had a single outlet in New York City, today it has five. It also has three distributors in Chicago. Lifeway obviously is at the forefront of commercial dairy foods.

We will soon learn recipes for newer and even tastier kefir drinks and kefir cheeses, specially designed to accomplish dietary goals like weight reduction without the necessity of nutritional deprivation. Meanwhile, if you know any additional data or unique kefir recipe that you want to share, or you have other useful comments or questions regarding kefir and kefir-making, feel free to email me at Guileless@msn.com or send me a facsimile message to my fax number (604) 421-3610 or, using the good old post office, write to me at 9566 Willowleaf Place, Burnaby, BC, V5A 4A5, Canada.

Alice ventured to taste it, and,
finding it very nice (it had, in fact,
a sort of mixed flavor of cherry-tart,
custard, pineapple, roast turkey, toffee,
and hot buttered toast),
she very soon finished it off.

ALICE'S ADVENTURES IN WONDERLAND

LEWIS CARROLL

Part IV

A WHIRL OF RECIPES

Chapter 8

Kefir Delights

A Whirl of Recipes

K efir is first and foremost a simple but wonderful thirst quencher, to which, however, you can easily add enhancing juices, jams, liqueurs, etc. Kefir is also suitable for flavoring soups, sauces, salads, raw vegetables, and it makes a great party dip! Moreover, wherever a recipe calls for milk, cream, buttermilk or yogurt, you may freely substitute kefir.

All the recipes can be prepared from homemade kefir, either freshly made to suit the recipe, or taken from refrigerated stock. Remember though that while you can use any quantity of milk to make kefir, the larger the amount of milk used, the longer it will take to curdle or "set." Also be aware that if you use too much milk it might go off before it ferments. If this should happen, remove the cone, wash the grains well under running water and start again, using less milk. If your kefir turns out thicker than anticipated, you can always thin it down with milk. In such cases I prefer to use skim milk for thinning it to the desired consistency.

To distinguish between thinner or softer kefir drinks and heartier kefir foods, I have used the titles "Softy Kefir" and "Creamy Kefir." By following these leads you will know the consistency of kefir required by the

61

recipe. In general, "soft" kefir looks a lot like buttermilk; "creamy" kefir has a consistency similar to quark.

The following recipes can either be copied exactly or taken as a departure point to your imagination. Be creative! And feel free to pass them among your friends and relatives. Always make sure, however, that the ingredients are not likely to cause an allergic reaction in people. It is a good idea to ask your guests if they have any serious allergies before serving any of the following dishes.

The recipes are designed to make a single portion, but the ingredients can easily be multiplied proportionately by the number of people being served, i.e., double the indicated quantities for two people, triple for three people, etc., and enjoy!

Softy Kefirs

Thirst Quenchers, Quick Snacks, Light Breakfasts, Lunches and Dinners

Adorable Apple Cereal

Take 2 oz (60 g) apples, 1 Tbsp. lemon juice, 1/2 oz (15 g) honey, 2 slices of white toast, 1/2 oz (15 g) finely chopped walnuts, 1/2 oz (15 g) almond paste, 7 oz (210 g) kefir. Grate apples and blend in lemon juice and honey. Crumble toast and mix in. Blend kefir with almond paste and pour over the mixture. Sprinkle with finely chopped walnuts and serve.

Amicable Almond Kefir Kocktail

Take 1 oz (30 g) almond paste, 1 cup kefir, 1 Tbsp. honey, and 1 Tbsp. wheat germ. Mix all ingredients. Season to taste. Serve.

Building Banana Kefir Shake

Take 1 egg yolk, 4 oz (100 g) banana, 4 oz (75 ml) kefir, and nutmeg for seasoning. Mix banana, egg yolk and kefir in blender or by hand. Put into tall glass. Add a little soda water. Sprinkle lightly with nutmeg.

Bonny Blackberry Refresher

Take 3/4 oz (20 g) oats, 3 Tbsp. water, a little honey to taste, 5 oz (150 g) blackberries in season, 2 oz (60 g) kefir, 1/4 oz (10 g) wheat germ, a handful of chopped almonds and Brazil nuts, crushed golden flaxseed. Soak oats overnight in water. Use 3 Tbsp. water per Tbsp. oats. In the morning mix the oats with honey, the slightly crushed blackberries and kefir. Put into a bowl and sprinkle with the chopped nuts.

Fruity Kefir Cool Drink

4 oz (125 ml) kefir, 4 oz (125 ml) mixed fruit juice. Shake or blend cooled kefir with fruit juice until foamy. Serve cold.

Honeyed Kefir Shake

Take 1 egg yolk, 4 oz (125 ml) kefir, 1 Tbsp. (10 g) honey, 2 Tbsp. (20 g) wheat germ. Thoroughly mix egg yolk, kefir, wheat germ and honey. Sprinkle lightly with nutmeg. Serve.

Karbonated Kefir Drink

4 oz (125 ml) kefir, 1 glass carbonated natural mineral water, 3 oz (75 g) fruit juice, 1 tsp. honey, and juice of 1/2 lemon. Thoroughly blend kefir, honey, fruit juice and lemon juice. Pour in mineral water. Stir until foamy. Serve immediately.

Marvelous Millet Soup

Take 8 oz (250 ml) kefir, 1/4 oz (10 g) honey, 1/2 oz (15 g) millet, a dash of cinnamon, 5 oz (150 g) fresh blueberries. Bring kefir to a boil. Add millet and let thicken. Sweeten with honey and flavor with cinnamon. Serve with the fresh, lightly pulped berries.

Nifty Nettle Kefir

Take 2 Tbsp. tender stinging nettle leaves (make sure you use gloves when handling fresh stinging nettles), 4 oz (125 ml) milk, 4 oz (125 ml) kefir, 1/2 oz (15 g) sugar or honey. Finely chop the leaves and scald with the milk brought to a boil. Afterwards blend milk and kefir, season with sweetener of your choice. Serve.

Nutty Professor Kefir Breakfast

Take 1 1/2 oz (40 g) chopped almonds and hazelnuts, 2 1/2 oz (75 ml) kefir, 4 oz (125 ml) buttermilk, 1/4 oz (10 g) honey, 1/2 oz (15 g) oats, juice of 1/2 lemon. Blend the kefir with buttermilk, honey and lemon juice until thick and creamy. Put into a bowl and sprinkle liberally with the chopped nuts. Roast the oats in a pan separately without fat. Sprinkle over all. Serve immediately.

Kefir Karot Kocktail

Take 4 oz (125 ml) kefir, 5 oz (150 g) carrots, 4 oz (125 ml) freshly squeezed orange juice, 1 tsp. lemon juice, 1 Tbsp. (10 g) honey. Put the washed carrots through juicer. Mix carrot juice with kefir, honey, orange juice and lemon juice. Season to taste with nutmeg.

Passionate Pear Oatmeal

Take 3/4 oz (20 g) oats, 3 Tbsp. water, 1 Tbsp. lemon juice, 1/2 oz (15 g) kefir, 1/4 oz (10 g) honey, 7 oz (200 g) fresh pears, 3/4 oz (20 g) grated almonds. Soak oats overnight in water. In the morning blend with lemon juice, kefir and honey. Grate pears and lightly blend into mixture. Sprinkle finished dish with almonds. Serve.

Peerless Pear Soup

Take 5 oz (150 g) pears, 4 oz (125 ml) kefir, 1 Tbsp. (10 g) flour, cinnamon, honey, cloves to taste. Peel pears and cut into pieces. Cook in a little water until soft. Add some water to flour and stir into a thick paste. Heat kefir with the cinnamon and cloves and stir in the flour paste. Bring to a boil. Sweeten with honey and add the pears. Serve.

Pithy Pit Fruit Kefir

Take 4 oz (100 g) stone fruit (plums, apricots, peaches, cherries), 1/2 oz (15 g) honey, 4 oz (125 ml) kefir, corn flakes, crumbled whole dark rye bread. Pit all fruit and cut into small pieces. Sweeten kefir with honey and beat until foamy. Pour over fruit. Sprinkle on bread crumbs. Enjoy.

Suave Raspberries with Strawberries

Take 4 oz (100 g) strawberries, 2 oz (50 g) raspberries (fresh, ripe, preferably locally grown), 4 oz (125 ml) kefir, 4 oz (125 ml) skim milk, 1 Tbsp. honey. Lightly blend the berries in a bowl, thoroughly mix kefir with milk and honey, gently pour over berries. A great summer treat!

Sweet Svelte Kefir

Take 8 oz (250 ml) kefir, lemon peel, 1/2 oz (15 g) honey, 1/2 oz (15 g) sago, 4 oz (100 g) strawberries. Clean and wash strawberries. Heat the kefir together with the lemon peel, add sago and let swell up. Mix honey into the finished brew. Serve with strawberries.

Sweet Woodruff Kefir

1 bundle sweet woodruff, 4 oz (125 ml) kefir, 1/4 oz (10 g) honey, 1/2 oz (15 g) chopped nuts, 1 oz (30 g) Graham whole wheat bread, 1/2 oz (15 g) golden raisins. Mix kefir and honey. Suspend sweet woodruff bundle in the kefir and let its flavor penetrate the kefir. Dice bread and put onto a soup plate. Pour the sweet woodruff kefir over the bread. Serve sprinkled with chopped nuts and raisins.

Wondrous Wheat Germ Soup

Take 8 oz (250 ml) soft kefir, 3/4 oz (20 g) grits (semolina), a little grated lemon peel, 1/2 oz (15 g) honey, 3/4 oz (20 g) raisins, 1/4 oz (10 g) wheat germ. Mix the semolina into the kefir, add the lemon peel and bring to a boil while constantly stirring. Stir in raisins and honey. Serve sprinkled with wheat germ.

Yummy Yeasty Rosehip Kocktail

Take 5 oz (150 g) kefir, 1/4 oz (10 g) nutritional yeast, 1/2 oz (15 g) mashed rosehip, 1 tsp. honey. Mix kefir with yeast and rosehip. Season to taste.

Creamy Kefirs

Snacks, Sumptuous Breakfasts, Lunches and Dinners

Apple and Pear Creamy Kefir

Take 3/4 oz (20 g) kefir, 1/4 oz (10 g) whipping cream, 4 oz (100 g) apples, 4 oz (100 g) pears, 1/4 oz (10 g) currants, 4 oz (125 ml) apple juice, 1/2 oz (15 g) honey. Thinly slice apples and pears. Place into bowl and sprinkle with currants. Mix honey and juice and pour over fruit. Lightly streak in kefir. Top decoratively with whipping cream. Serve.

Artful Creamy Kefir

Take 4 oz (100 g) kefir, 1 Tbsp. skim milk, 1 tomato, 1 Tbsp. mixed herbs, 1 tsp. capers, 5 black olives. Stir milk and kefir together. Blend in the herbs, finely chopped tomato, capers and the whole olives minus pit. Season to taste. Serve.

Caraway Potatoes and Red Cabbage Salad

1. Take 8 oz (250 g) potatoes, 1/2 oz (15 g) European cultured creamery butter, 1/2 tsp. caraway seed, 4 oz (125 ml) kefir. Peel and dice potatoes. Melt the butter in a suitable casserole. Add the potatoes and sprinkle with caraway seeds. Add boiling hot kefir. Cook potatoes in oven at high heat until the potatoes have soaked up all the milky liquid.

2. Take 7 oz (200 g) red cabbage, 1 raw apple, 1 medium-sized onion, 1 bay leaf, 2 ripe juniper berries, 1/4 tsp. cloves. 1 garlic clove, 1/2 oz (15 g) cold-pressed flax oil, 1 tsp. lemon juice, herbs and honey to taste. Cook red cabbage in minimal water. Add grated apple, bay leaf, cloves, juniper berries, peeled onion and crushed garlic clove and continue to cook until tender. Remove excess liquid through strainer and let cool. Grate apple. Now blend in oil and lemon juice and season with honey and herbs. Let saturate well before serving.

Berry Potpourri Kefir

Take 4 oz (125 g) fresh mixed berries (red currant, black currant, gooseberries, blueberries, raspberries), 4 oz (125 ml) kefir, honey to taste, dark rye bread crumbs and vanilla to taste. Clean berries and place in bowl. Sweeten kefir with honey and season with vanilla. Pour over berries. Sprinkle with dark rye bread crumbs. Serve cold.

Bluish Blueberry Creamy Kefir

Take 4 oz (100 g) kefir, 5 oz (150 g) fresh blueberries, 3/4 oz (20 g) honey, 3/4 oz (20 g) bread crumbs, 2 Tbsp. blueberry yogurt. Stir kefir, honey, milk and yogurt into a foamy bluish cream. Sprinkle bread crumbs into a flat bottomed bowl, add washed and drained blueberries, cover with kefir cream. Scatter a few choice blueberries over top. Serve.

Bold Banana Boat

Take 4 oz (100 g) kefir, 4 oz (100 g) ripe mashed banana, a few ripe strawberries and pineapple sections, 1/2 oz lemon, 1/2 oz (15 g) honey, 1 tsp. chopped fresh mint. Thoroughly blend banana mash with lemon and honey using a fork. Gently streak into kefir. Place into elongated glass dish. Decorate with strawberries and pineapple. Season lightly with fresh mint. Enjoy!

Candid Carrot Creamy Kefir

Take 5 oz (150 g) carrots, 1/4 apple, 1 tsp. lemon juice, herbs to taste, 2 oz (60 g) kefir, 1 tsp. honey, 1 shallot, 1/4 oz (10 g) chopped nuts. Clean carrots and apple and grate both into a bowl. Mix well with lemon juice, herbs, honey, grated shallot and 1 Tbsp. kefir. Cover mixture with remaining kefir and sprinkle liberally with nuts.

Charming Cherry Creamy Kefir

Take 5 oz (150 g) cherries, 4 oz (125 ml) kefir, 1/2 oz (15 g) honey, vanilla sugar to taste, 1/4 oz (10 g) semolina, 1 free range chicken egg. Pit cherries. Steam in a bit of water. Add vanilla sugar to kefir and heat to a boil. Add semolina and simmer until thickened. Mix in honey and cherries. Stir in egg yolk. Beat, then fold in the stiffened egg white. Let cool. Serve.

Cherry Kefir Soufflé

Take 8 oz (250 g) fresh cherries, 3/4 oz (20 g) European cultured creamery butter, 3/4 oz (20 g) honey, 1 tsp. powdered cinnamon, 1 free range chicken egg, 1 1/2 German rolls, 3 Tbsp. kefir. Pit cherries. Mix egg yolk and kefir. Soak the diced rolls in this mix. Beat butter, honey and cinnamon to a foamy consistency. Press moisture out of rolls and add to mixture. Beat egg white until stiff and fold into the cherries. Pour the soufflé into a oiled, fireproof casserole and bake at medium heat.

Cool Carrot Creamy Kefir

Take 4 oz (100 g) kefir, 1 Tbsp. honey, 1 tsp. lime juice, 4 oz (100 g) carrots. Finely grate clean carrots. Blend lime juice and honey. Mix all into the kefir and season to taste.

Cucumber with Kefir Mushrooms and Tomato Sauce

1. Take 1 cucumber, 1 red onion, 5 oz (150 g) mushrooms, 1 Tbsp. chopped mixed herbs, 1 tsp. lemon juice, 3/4 oz (20 g) European cultured creamery butter, 2 oz (60 g) kefir. Remove skin from cucumber, cut in half, scrape out all seed matter. Season inside with finely diced onion and lemon juice. Clean mushrooms, dice and mix with remaining lemon juice, kefir and herbs. Fill cucumber with this mixture. Sprinkle with small flakes cut from hard butter. Cook in oven with a little water for 30 minutes. Serve with tomato sauce and potatoes in their skins.

2. Tomato sauce: Take 5 oz (150 g) ripe tomatoes, 1/4 oz (10 g) flour, 1/4 oz (10 g) European cultured creamery butter, 2 Tbsp. kefir, pepper to taste. Skin tomatoes and puree. Mix flour into butter and lightly brown. Add kefir and tomato juice and bring to a boil. Season the sauce with herbs to taste. Serve with the above.

Elegant Egg Creamy Kefir Potatoes and Wild Veggies

1. Take 4 oz (100 g) potatoes, 1 hard boiled egg, 4 oz (100 g) ripe tomatoes, 1/4 Tbsp. chopped parsley, 1 shallot, 1/4 oz (10 g) European cultured creamery butter, 2 1/2 oz (75 ml) kefir. Finely dice potatoes, egg and tomatoes. Layer into a greased casserole. Sprinkle onions and parsley over each layer. Pour kefir over all. Cover with small flakes cut from the cold butter. Bake in oven for 1/2 hour.

2. Salad: Take 4 oz (100 g) mixed leaves of watercress, dandelion, sorrel (if available also use coltsfoot, greater plantain, ground ivy, ripwort plantain), 1/4 oz (10 g) cold-pressed flaxseed oil, 1 tsp. lemon juice, 1 tsp. honey, 1 small shallot, 1 garlic clove. Carefully wash leaves and drip dry in a strainer. Make dressing by blending the oil with the lemon juice, honey, finely diced garlic and shallot. Pour over leaves at the table. Eat immediately.

Flaky Kefir Pastry Cookies

Take 8 oz (250 g) flour, 8 oz (250 ml) kefir, 8 oz (250 g) European cultured creamery butter, 12 oz (350 g) fruit filling, 1 egg yolk, 1 oz (30 g) icing sugar. Knead flour with kefir and butter. Let stand for one hour in a cool place, then roll out. Cut out cookies (any shape or form) and cover with fruit (or jam). Fold together. Push together well. Baste with egg yolk and bake in oven. Sprinkle with icing sugar and serve warm or cold.

Flaxseed Kefir Spread

Take 4 oz (125 ml) kefir, 1 1/4 oz (40 g) cold-pressed flaxseed oil, 3/4 oz (25 ml) skim milk, 1/4 oz (10 g) diced radishes, 1/4 oz (10 g) diced tomatoes, 1/4 oz (10 g) diced pickles, 1/4 oz (10 g) capers, 1/4 oz (10 g) caraway seeds. Mix kefir with oil and milk in the blender or with eggbeater until creamy. Stir in the remaining ingredients.

Fresh Fruit Salad with Kefir

Take 4 oz (100 g) apples, 4 oz (100 g) oranges, 2 oz (60 g) bananas, 1/2 oz (15 g) raisins, 1/2 oz (15 g) grated hazel nuts, 2 oz (60 g) kefir, 1/2 oz (15 g) honey. Skin and dice fruit and mix in honey, nuts and kefir.

Hale Herb Creamy Kefir

Take 4 oz (100 g) low fat kefir, 2 Tbsp. skim milk, 1 Tbsp. mixed herbs, 1 small shallot, 1 tsp. lemon juice, 1 tsp. honey. Mix kefir with milk, honey, grated shallot, lemon juice and herbs. Season and serve.

Healthful Honey Creamy Kefir

Take 4 oz (100 g) kefir, 3/4 oz (20 g) honey, 1 Tbsp. skim milk, 1 dash cinnamon, 10 drops lemon juice. Thoroughly blend kefir with honey, cinnamon, milk and lemon juice. Season to taste. Serve.

Hearty Horseradish Creamy Kefir

Take 4 oz (100 g) kefir, 2 Tbsp. sour cream, 1 medium-sized grated apple, 1 Tbsp. grated horseradish, 1 tsp. lime juice, 1 Tbsp. honey. Thoroughly blend kefir, cream and honey, then lightly stir in the grated apple and horseradish. Season to taste. Serve.

Honorable Horseradish Triple Kefir Dumplings

1. Kefir Dumplings: Take 4 oz (125 ml) kefir, 1 free range chicken egg, 2 oz (60 g) corn flakes, 4 oz (100 g) peeled, grated cooked potatoes, 1 Tbsp. chopped mixed herbs. Blend the kefir with the egg, corn flakes and potatoes in a mixer. Season with herbs and let stand for 15 minutes. Cut off small dumplings using a spoon. Cook in boiling water. Lift out with skimmer.

2. Kefir Sauce: Take 4 oz (125 ml) kefir, 1/4 oz (10 g) European cultured creamery butter, 1/4 oz (10 g) flour, 1/2 egg yolk, 1/4 apple, grated horseradish, lemon juice and honey to taste. Lightly brown the flour in butter, add kefir and bring to boil. Take from stove and mix in grated horseradish and grated apple. Season with lemon juice and honey. Smooth in egg yolk. Serve over dumplings.

3. Kefir Salad Dressing: Take 1 oz (30 g) kefir, 1 Tbsp. flaxseed oil, 1 tsp. lemon juice, spices and herbs to taste. Blend all together and season to taste.

Makes a delicious full course dinner. Of course, the kefir salad dressing and kefir sauce can be used in other suitable salads and dishes. Bon appetite!

Horseradish Spread

Take 4 oz (100 g) horseradish, 4 fl oz (125 ml) kefir, 1 oz (30 g) European cultured creamery butter, 1/2 apple. Beat butter until foamy. Grate apple and fold in. Add horseradish and mix. Add kefir and stir in. Spread on your favorite bread as is or season with herbs and spices to taste.

Juniper Kefir

Take 4 oz (100 g) juniper berries, a little water, 1 tsp. grated lemon peel from cleaned, unsprayed (organically grown) lemon, 1/2 oz (15 g) honey, 3/4 oz (20 g) cornstarch, 3 Tbsp. kefir, 4 oz (100 g) steamed apple slices. Cook juniper berries in water with lemon peel and pass through a strainer. Sweeten the juniper pulp with honey and bring back to a boil. Mix cornstarch into kefir and add. Boil again. Place apple slices into a bowl and cover with the juniper kefir.

Kefir Roast with Romaine

1. Take 125 ml kefir, 2 Tbsp. skim milk, 1 Tbsp. whipping cream, 1 free range chicken egg, 2 oz (50 g) crumbled dark rye bread, caraway seeds and sage to taste, 1 onion, 1/4 oz (10 g) European cultured creamery butter and 10 g bread crumbs. Mix kefir with cream and milk in blender. Stir in rye bread crumbs. Add caraway seeds, grated onion and sage. Transfer to a small greased oven dish. Cover the surface with cream and let your kefir roast cook in the oven for 30 minutes.

2. Take 8 oz (250 g) Romaine lettuce, 1/2 oz (20 g) European cultured creamery butter, 1 onion, 1/2 oz (20 g) flour, 4 oz (125 ml) kefir, 1 free range chicken egg yolk, 1 tsp. lemon juice, 7 oz (200 g) potatoes. Wash the Romaine well. While still wet steam in covered pot. Finely chop. Melt butter. Sauté the chopped onions in the butter and sprinkle with flour. Add kefir. Let cook and season with lemon juice and egg yolk. Mix in the chopped Romaine and serve with potatoes cooked in their skins and the above roast.

Leek Kefir Potatoes

Take 8 oz (250 g) leeks, 8 oz (250 g) potatoes, 3 oz (75 g) Parmesan cheese, 3/4 oz (20 g) European cultured creamery butter, 1 tsp. chopped parsley, 1 tsp. paprika, 1/2 cup kefir, 1/2 cup vegetable broth. Carefully clean leek, removing all impurities. Cut into thin slices and pile in layers into a casserole. Stir kefir, paprika and parsley into the vegetable broth. Pour the thoroughly stirred mix over the leeks. Cut cold butter into tiny flakes and sprinkle it and the grated Parmesan cheese over the soufflé. Bake in oven until leeks are soft.

Lemon Kefir

Take 3 oz (75 g) kefir, 1 tsp. lemon juice, 1 tsp. grated lemon peel from cleaned, unsprayed (organically grown) lemon, 1/2 oz (15 g) honey, 1 Tbsp. skim milk, 1 Tbsp. whipping cream. Blend the kefir with the lemon juice, milk and cream. Serve.

Lovely Leeks with Roasted Potatoes

1. Take 8 oz (250 g) leek, 1/4 oz (10 g) European cultured creamery butter, 1/4 oz (10 g) flour, 2 oz (60 g) kefir, 1/2 oz (15 g) grated Parmesan cheese, nutmeg to garnish. Carefully clean leek to remove all impurities. Cut into long, thin strips and cook in a little water until soft. Add butter. Slowly add flour to kefir, stirring constantly. Add the mixture to the leek broth as a thickening agent. Season with cheese and nutmeg and serve with roast potatoes.

2. Roast potatoes: Take 7 oz (200 g) potatoes, 3/4 oz (20 g) cold-pressed olive oil, 1 small red onion. Peel potatoes and slice thinly. Heat the oil and sauté the potatoes until crispy brown, sprinkling the finely diced onions during the sautéing.

Magical Mushroom Kefir Spread

Take 4 oz (125 ml) kefir, 1/2 oz (20 g) European cultured creamery butter, 1 tsp. chopped parsley, 4 oz (100 g) braised mushrooms, 1 Tbsp. honey, 1 Tbsp. lemon juice. Whip butter and kefir until foamy. Finely chop the mushrooms and mix with parsley. Season with honey and lemon juice. Add herbs to taste.

Mushroom Kefir Dogs

Take 4 oz (100 g) braised mushroom, 1/2 oz (15 g) flour, 1/2 oz (15 g)

European cultured creamery butter, 1 oz (30 ml) skim milk, 1 oz (30 ml) kefir, 1/4 oz (10 g) cold-pressed extra virgin olive oil, 1/4 oz (10 g) whole wheat bread crumbs, 1 free range chicken egg, 1 tsp. chopped parsley. Brown the flour in butter, add milk, bring to a boil and cook until thickened. Add kefir. Drain the mushrooms and chop finely. Mix with the chopped parsley. Knead mass into sausage-like forms. Mix egg and bread crumbs. Roll the "sausages" in this mixture. Sauté in hot oil until browned.

Nighttime Nut Creamy Kefir

Take 4 oz (100 g) low fat kefir, 2 oz (50 g) mixed nuts, 1 Tbsp. skim milk, 1/2 oz (15 g) honey. Stir honey and milk into kefir. Lightly roast coarsely chopped nuts in a frying pan and stir into mixture. Season to taste. Enjoy a nightcap treat!

Orange Kefir Shake

Take 4 oz (125 ml) kefir, 1 orange, 1/2 oz (15 g) honey. Press out orange juice. Blend all ingredients in mixer. Serve immediately.

Peppermint Kefir

Take 1 1/2 oz (40 g) semolina, 3 oz (75 ml) kefir, 2 oz (60 ml) skim milk, 1 Tbsp. honey, 2 tsp. finely chopped peppermint leaves. Bring milk and kefir to a boil. Add semolina and honey and cook until thickened. When the grits are ready, fold in the peppermint leaves. Fill dessert bowl rinsed out with cold water. Invert bowl onto serving dish. Serve covered in fruit juice.

Preeminent Kefir Potatoes with Kefir Bean Salad

1. Potatoes: Take 8 oz (250 g) boiled potatoes, 4 oz (125 ml) kefir, 2 free range chicken eggs, 1 small red onion, caraway seeds, 1 Tbsp. chopped mixed herbs. Grate the peeled and cooked potatoes. Blend kefir with eggs, grated onion, caraway seeds and herbs. Put into casserole and grill with top heat at medium setting.

2. Bean Salad: Take 7 oz (200 g) green beans, 1 twig savory, 1/4 oz cold-pressed oil (olive, flax, etc.), 1 tsp. lemon juice, 1 tsp. honey, herbs to taste, 1 tsp. chopped parsley, 1 oz (30 g) kefir. String beans and cut into sections. Cook until soft in a minimal amount of water. Stir kefir with oil, lemon juice, chopped parsley, honey and herbs. Fold in the cool beans. Let soak in before serving.

Perky Plums with Kefir

Take 4 oz (125 ml) kefir, 4 oz (100 g) plums, 1/2 oz (15 g) honey, 2 Tbsp. skim milk, 1 Tbsp. lemon juice. Blend kefir with milk and honey. Pit plums and finely dice or blend to mash. Fold into kefir mix and season with a few drops of lemon juice.

Red Kefir Kurrant Soufflé

Take 1 cup thick red currant compote, 2 oz (60 g) dark whole rye bread crumbs, 3 Tbsp. kefir, 1 free range chicken egg, dash cinnamon, 1/2 oz (15 g) honey. Layer compote and bread crumbs into small ovenproof bowl. Mix egg with kefir, cinnamon and honey and pour over the soufflé. Bake at medium heat. A real treat!

Red Kefir Beets with Pickles and Potatoes

Take 8 oz (250 g) red beets, 1 large soured or salt pickle, 1/2 oz (15 g) European cultured creamery butter, 2 oz (60 g) kefir, 1/2 oz (15 g) flour, ground caraway and rosemary for garnish, 1 Tbsp. honey, 1 Tbsp. lemon juice, 7 oz (200 g) potatoes. Peel the beets, cut into thin slices. Simmer in a little water. Slowly add flour into kefir while stirring. Add thickened kefir to beets. Mix in butter, caraway, rosemary, honey, lemon juice and the grated or finely diced pickle. Serve with potatoes boiled in their skins.

Sumptuous Sorrel Soufflé with Kefir Salad

1. Take 2 dried German split rolls, 1 free range chicken egg, 2 oz (60 ml) skim milk, 2 oz (60 ml) kefir, 1/4 oz (10 g) sorrel, 1/2 oz (15 g) grated Parmesan cheese, 1 Tbsp. European cultured creamery butter for greasing. Dice rolls and soak in mixture of kefir and milk. Then mix in egg and chopped sorrel. Place in greased casserole. Sprinkle with cheese. Bake.

2. Salad: Take 2 oz (75 ml) kefir, 2 oz (60 g) apples, 5 oz (150 g) celery root, 1 tsp. lemon juice, 3 Tbsp. whipping cream, 1/2 oz (15 g) nut butter. Beat kefir and cream until foamy. Skin apples and celery root. Coarsely grate both. Mix with the kefir and cream. Season with lemon juice and nut butter. Add herbs to taste.

Spirited Spinach Kefir

Take 5 oz (150 g) fresh raw spinach, 1 egg yolk, 2 oz (60 g) kefir, herbs and lemon juice to taste. Wash spinach well. Let drip dry in a strainer. Stir the kefir, egg yolk, herbs and lemon juice into a smooth sauce and pour over the spinach leaves. Serve.

Strapping Strawberries with Nut Butter

Take 5 oz (150 g) very ripe strawberries, 1/4 oz (10 g) nut butter, 4 oz (125 ml) kefir, cereal and honey to taste. Press berries through a strainer. Mix the resulting soft strawberry mass with the nut butter and the kefir. Sweeten with honey and decorate with sprinkled-on cereal. A body builder!

Strawberry Kefir Shake

Take 2 oz (60 g) ripe strawberries, 1/2 oz (15 g) honey, 4 oz (125 ml) kefir. Blend all ingredients in mixer or crush strawberries and blend with egg-beater.

Super Sweet Creamy Kefir

Take 4 oz (100 g) kefir, 2 Tbsp. skim milk, 2 Tbsp. mixed and mashed fruit, 1 oz (30 g) raspberry jelly, 1 tsp. lemon juice, 1 Tbsp. liquid honey. Mix the kefir with the mashed fruit and jelly. Add lemon juice. Add honey for extra sweetness.

Tomatoes and Cucumber on Kefir Rice

1. Take 7 oz (200 g) ripe tomatoes, 7 oz (200 g) fresh cucumber, 3/4 oz (20 g) European cultured creamery butter, 1 red onion, 1 tsp. chopped dill, mixed herbs for seasoning, paprika, 2 oz (60 g) kefir, 1/2 oz (15 g) flour. Melt butter in pan, slightly roast onions in the butter. Add peeled and diced cucumber. Sauté to near ready until cucumber is soft. Meanwhile remove skin from tomatoes and cut each tomato into eight sections. Add to frying pan together with herbs and paprika. Mix flour with the kefir. Stir into tomato mixture and cook until thickened. Sprinkle with dill and serve on a bed of rice.

2. Kefir Rice: Take 1 oz (30 g) long grained rice, 1/4 (10 g) wild rice, 4 oz (125 ml) vegetable broth, 1 tsp. chopped parsley, 1/4 oz (10 g) European cultured creamery butter, 3/4 oz (20 ml) kefir. Pour rice into boiling broth and cook over low heat in covered pot until ready. Mix kefir, melted butter and parsley. Stir into rice. Serve with the above.

Tonic Tomato Creamy Kefir

Take 7 oz (200 g) tomatoes, 1 red onion, 1 tsp. fresh chives, 2 oz (60 ml) kefir, herbs to season, 1 tsp. honey, 1 tsp. lemon juice. Slice tomatoes and onion and decoratively place on plate. Mix kefir with herbs and honey. Pour over tomato/onion arrangement. Sprinkle with finely chopped chives and serve.

Total Tomato Creamy Kefir

Take 5 oz (150 g) Creamy kefir, 1 Tbsp. skim milk, 1 small shallot, 1 tsp. chopped fresh parsley, 2 ripe tomatoes. Puree tomatoes in blender or skin and finely chop. Mix with kefir and add grated shallot and 3/4 of the chopped parsley. Garnish with remaining parsley. Serve as appetizer or main course.

Winning Watercress Creamy Kefir

Take 4 oz (100 g) kefir, 1 tsp. lemon juice, 1 ripe tomato, 1 Tbsp. chopped watercress, 1 Tbsp. skim milk. Blend kefir with milk, lemon juice, watercress, skinned and diced tomato and season to taste. Serve.

Kool Kefir Cheeses

Snacks, Sumptuous Breakfasts, Lunches and Dinners

Belgian Endives and Kefir Cheese Offering

Take 2 fresh Belgian endives, 4 oz (100 g) kefir cheese, 1/4 oz (10 g) chopped walnuts, 1 tomato. Carefully wash endives. Slice endives and tomato. Add cheese. Gently mix all ingredients. Season to taste with lemon juice and honey. Serve as appetizer.

Brochette of Broccoli with Kefir Cheese Sauce

Take 4 oz (100 g) broccoli, 1/2 oz (10 g) European cultured creamery butter, 3/4 oz (20 g) grated Parmesan cheese, 3/4 oz (20 g) crumbled kefir cheese, 1/2 oz (10 g) flour, 2 oz (75 ml) kefir, 2 oz (75 ml) skim milk, 1 hard-boiled free range chicken egg, dash nutmeg. Wash broccoli. Place on a skewer and cook briefly in a bit of water. Do not overcook! Separately brown flour in butter. Add the broccoli water to this, then add milk and liquid kefir. Mix cheeses into this sauce and season with nutmeg. Pour over skewer and serve surrounded by quartered egg.

Klaus' Koolest Kefir Käse

Take 2 oz (60 g) kefir cheese, 1 ripe, preferably homegrown tomato, 1 tsp. chopped dill, 1 fresh Anjou pear slice, 1/4 oz (10 g) European cultured creamery butter. Whip butter until foamy. Add kefir cheese and stir in skinned, diced tomato, chopped dill and grated pear. Season to taste and serve. Koolest!

Kefir Cheese Herb Spread

Take 1 oz (30 g) kefir cheese, 1 free range egg yolk, 1/4 oz (10 g) flour, 4 oz (125 ml) liquid kefir, 3/4 oz (20 g) European cultured creamery butter, herbs and spices. Add kefir cheese. Mix flour with egg yolk and fold into kefir cheese. Add liquid kefir and heat until thickened. Remove from heat. Add butter and seasonings to taste.

Now that you have experienced how truly versatile kefir is in cooking, you will no doubt begin to dream up even tastier kefir dishes on your own. If they are truly mouthwatering, let me know and I will give them a try and perhaps include them in a revised edition of this book. Remember the myriad uses kefir has in food preparation: It provides the base for great flavored shakes, tasty and healthy salad dressings. Kefir cheese (either with quark-like consistency or further ripened) is a wonderful addition to any meal and makes a fitting finale to a great dinner.

Santé et bon appetite.

Endnotes

1. Dem Herrlichsten, was auch der Geist empfangen,
    Drängt immer fremd und fremder Stoff sich an;
    Wenn wir zum Guten dieser Welt gelangen,
    Dann heiflt das Beßre Trug und Wahn.
    Goethe - translated by Klaus Kaufmann from *Faust 1, 634-639*

2. My source book has printed "1990s," however, this was obviously a printing error.

3. Chaitow & Trenev, 1990, Koroleva, 1988. (*Kefir: A Literature Review* by Dawn C. Grassick and John A. Menzies)

4. Kosikowski 1977

5. Koroleva, 1988a, Steinkraus, et al, 1983; and others. (*Kefir: A Literature Review* by Dawn C. Grassick and John A. Menzies)

6. *Der Murks mit der Milch*, 1994, emu-Verlags GmbH, Lahnstein, Germany

7. As described in my book *Silica – The Amazing Gel*, Pasteur with true prophetic vision, called attention to the importance that silica would have one day in human nutrition!

8. The authors of *ProBiotics*, The revolutionary "friendly bacteria" way to vital health and well-being.

9. Chaitow, Leon, ND, DO and Natasha Trenev, *Probiotics*, 1990, Thorsons Publisher, Wellingborough, England

10. According to Johannes Kuhl, MD, PhD and E. Schneider, MD

11. Harry Seneca, MDet al, as reported by B. Hunter

12. Oberman, 1985, (*Kefir: A Literature Review* by Dawn C. Grassick and John A. Menzies)

13. Koroleva, 1991, (*Kefir: A Literature* Review by Dawn C. Grassick and John A. Menzies)

14. WWW, page: Benefits to Health, The Goodlife Company and Friends, August 16, 1996

15. WWW, page: Benefits to Health, The Goodlife Company and Friends, August 16, 1996

16. Chaitow, Leon, ND, DO and Natasha Trenev, *Probiotics*, 1990, Thorsons Publisher, Wellingborough, England

---

Bibliography

Bruker, Dr. med M. O. and Dr. phil. Mathias Jung. 1994. *Der Murks mit der Milch*. Lahnstein, Germany: emu-Verlags-GmbH.

Chaitow, Leon, and Natasha Trenev. 1990. *ProBiotics*. Wellingborough, England: Thorsons.

Flake, Jr., Lue Dean. 1976. *Kitchen Cheesemaking*. Harrisburg, PA.: Stackpole.

Grassick, Dawn C., and John A. Menzies. 1996. *Kefir: A Literature Review*. (unpublished)

Helferich, W., and Dennis Westhoff 1980. *All About Yogurt.* Englewood Cliffs, NJ: Prentice-Hall.

Krebs, Susanna, and Gusti Pollak. 1995. *Kefir: Der Alleskinner in der Küche.* Aarau, Switzerland: AT Verlag.

Meixner, Axel. 1982, 1984. *Der Kefirpilz.* Stuttgart, Germany: AT Verlag.

Prescott, Samuel Cate, and Cecil Gordon Dunn, Cecil Gordon. 1982. *Prescott and Dunn's Industrial Microbiology.* Westport, CN: Avi Publishing.

Trum Hunter, Beatrice. 1973. *Yogurt, Kefir and Other Milk Cultures.* New Canaan, CN: Keats.

Trum Hunter, Beatrice. 1973. *Fermented Foods and Beverages: An Old Tradition.* New Canaan, CN: Keats.

Volz, Gerda. 1996. *Rezepte mit Joghurt, Kefir and Co.* Niedernhausen, Germany: Falken Verlag.

Useful Addresses

Alive Academy of Nutrition
7436 Fraser Park Dr.
Burnaby BC V5J 5B9
Canada
604-435-1919
Fax: 604-435-4888

Alta Dena Certified Dairy
City of Industry CA 91744
USA
800-MILK-123

Avalon Dairy Ltd.
5805 Wales Street
Vancouver BC
V5R 3N5
Canada
604-434-2434
Fax: 604-434-4227

Lifeway Food Inc.
7625 N. Austin Ave.
Skokie IL 60077
USA
847-967-1010
Fax: 847-967-6558
Internet: http://www.lifeway.com

Teldon of Canada Ltd.
7436 Fraser Park Dr.
Burnaby BC V5J 5B9
Canada
800-663-2212
604-436-3312
Fax: 604-435-4862

The Goodlife Company and Friends Pty. Ltd.
36-38 Central Drive
Andrews Qld. 4220
Australia
011-61-7-5593-8744
Fax: 011-61-7-5593-8316
Email:
goodlife@OntheNet.com.au
Internet:
HTTP:/WWW.nt.com.au/goodlife

Index

A

abdominal pains, 10
acetic acid, 13, 19
acetylcholine, 32
acidophilus, 55
Adorable Apple Cereal, 62
age spots, 50
aging, 19
alcohol, 5, 9-10, 16, 18, 32, 38, 47
allergic conditions, 35
allergies, 35, 49, 62
alpha hydroxy acid, 50
Amicable Almond, 62
amino acids, 17
antibiotic, 13, 34-35
appetite, 35, 70
Apple and Pear Creamy Kefir, 51, 62, 65-67, 69-70
Artful Creamy Kefir, 65
arthritic, 35

B

B-vitamins, 32
bacilli, 11, 18-19
bactericidal, 13, 34
bacteriocin, 54
bacteriocins, 13
bacteriolysins, 54
beer, 5, 16-17
Belgian Endives and Kefir Cheese Offering, 75
Berry Potpourri Kefir, 66

bifido, 19
bile salts, 54
Bluish Blueberry Creamy Kefir, 66
Bold Banana Boat, 66
Bonny Blackberry Refresher, 62
Brochette of Broccoli with Kefir Cheese Sauce, 75
budding, 16
Building Banana 62
buttermilk, 4, 7, 11, 37, 43, 47-48, 61-63

C

C. kefyr, 17
C. pseudotropicalis, 17
calcium, 36, 56
cancer, 9, 17, 26, 31-34
Candid Carrot Creamy Kefir, 67
Candida albicans, 15, 17, 55
Candida, 15, 17, 55
Caraway Potatoes and Red Cabbage Salad, 66
carbohydrate, 6, 10, 32
carbon, 5, 16-17, 25, 32, 39-40, 47
carbon dioxide, 5, 16, 32, 39-40, 47
carbonic acid, 27, 32
casein, 6, 9, 12
catabolism, 24
catalysis, 24
cell proliferation, 17
certified raw milk, 5-6, 13, 39

Recommended Reading

Kombucha Rediscovered! by Klaus Kaufmann

ProBiotics by Leon Chaitow

How to Fight Cancer and Win by William L. Fischer

Making Sauerkraut and Pickled Vegetables at Home by Annelies Schoeneck